STARK

KOMPAKT-WISSEN
ENGLISCH

Rainer Jacob

Prüfungswortschatz

Realschule

Umschlagbild
Gestaltungselement Flagge: © Carsten Reisinger – Fotolia.com

© 2016 Stark Verlag GmbH
www.stark-verlag.de

Inhalt

Vorwort

Liebe Schülerin, lieber Schüler,

du hast sicher schon gemerkt, wie wichtig Vokabeln im Englischunterricht sind. Egal ob es darum geht, einen Text richtig zu verstehen, Fragen zu beantworten, einen Brief oder sonstigen Text zu verfassen – immer brauchst du einen umfangreichen Wortschatz. Damit du sicher und gut gerüstet in Klassenarbeiten und in deine Realschulabschlussprüfung gehen kannst, bietet dir dieser Band doppelte Hilfe an.

- Zum einen sind die Vokabeln zu den wichtigsten Themen, die im Unterricht behandelt werden, übersichtlich in einzelnen Kapiteln zusammengestellt. Auf diese Weise lassen sie sich leichter lernen. Außer der deutschen Bedeutung des Wortes findest du auch einen Beispielsatz: Erst durch die Verwendung des Wortes in einem sinnvollen Zusammenhang wird dir klar, wie du das Wort anwenden kannst. Hier kannst du auch Synonyme und Antonyme nachsehen.

- Zum anderen enthält der Band eine alphabetische Liste mit wichtigen Wörtern. Dort kannst du Wörter, die du (noch) nicht kennst, nachschlagen, um sie dann zu lernen und in deinen Wortschatz aufzunehmen.

Viel Erfolg für deine Klassenarbeiten und die Realschulabschlussprüfung!

Rainer Jacob

Abkürzungsverzeichnis

AE	American English
BE	British English
a.m.	vormittags
p.m.	nachmittags
jmdm.	jemandem
jmdn.	jemanden
Pl.	Plural
s.o.	someone
sth.	something
=	Synonym (syn)
≠	Antonym / Gegenteil (opp = opposite)
[I]	Lautschrift, die erklärt, wie ein Wort ausgesprochen wird

Around the World

vocabulary	dt. Bedeutung	English sentence	syn/opp
abroad	*ins/im Ausland*	A lot of young people go abroad in order to learn foreign languages.	= overseas
accommodation	*Unterkunft*	Most travellers book their accommodation (hotels, youth hostels, etc.) online.	
(to) afford	*sich etwas leisten (können)*	My parents will lend me the money, otherwise I couldn't afford the trip to Cambridge.	
(to) amaze **amazement**	*erstaunen* *Erstaunen*	We were amazed at how friendly and helpful the staff were.	
amazing	*erstaunlich*	The landscape was really amazing – there were tall mountains and beautiful sandy beaches.	= astonishing
apartment [AE]	*Wohnung*	We spent five days in Gerry's apartment in Chicago.	= flat [BE]
(to) apply **application**	*beantragen, sich bewerben* *Bewerbung*	If you need a visa, you should apply early.	
arrival	*Ankunft*	On our arrival we were greeted by our host family.	≠ departure
(to) arrive	*ankommen*		≠ (to) leave
(to) attempt **attempt**	*versuchen* *Versuch*	An American scientific team attempted to find the Loch Ness Monster.	= (to) try hard, (to) make an effort

vocabulary	dt. Bedeutung	English sentence	syn/opp
(to) attract **attractive**	*anziehen* *attraktiv, anziehend*	Today many tourists are attracted by the wax figures in Madame Tussauds.	
(to) avoid	*vermeiden*	It is good to get to the airport in time in order to avoid problems.	
bed and breakfast	*Übernachtung mit Frühstück*	In England you can find a lot of places which offer bed and breakfast.	= B&B
(to) board	*an Bord gehen, einsteigen*	We still have two hours left before we have to board our plane.	≠ (to) get off, (to) disembark
boarding house	*Pension*	The hotels were all really expensive, so we stayed at a boarding house instead.	
(to) book	*buchen*	I always book my holiday at the last minute.	
booking	*Reservierung, Buchung*	The hotel manager is happy about the number of bookings during the summer months.	
(to) borrow	*(aus-)leihen, entleihen*	In many seaside resorts, you can borrow surfing and diving equipment.	
busy	*belebt*	Oxford Street is extremely busy at Christmas shopping time.	
(to) camp **camping**	*zelten, lagern* *Camping, Zelten*	We still need a new tent and mosquito spray before we can camp by the lake.	
campsite	*Campingplatz*	A campsite is the place where people can park their camper vans or put up their tents.	= camping ground [AE]

vocabulary	dt. Bedeutung	English sentence	syn/opp
camping van	Wohnmobil	Our camping van is really comfortable – it has two beds, a small kitchen and a shower.	
capital	Hauptstadt	The capital of the USA is Washington, D.C.	
(to) cash	einlösen	Mr Smith cashed a £100 cheque at Barclays Bank.	
(to) check in	sich anmelden	We checked in at our hotel in the afternoon.	≠ (to) check out
climate	Klima	The climate in Scotland is said to be cool and rainy.	
coast	Küste	The USA is about 2,800 miles wide from coast to coast.	
comfortable	bequem	Our seats on the plane were very comfortable.	≠ uncomfortable
comfort	Komfort		
(to) comment	sich äußern, einen Kommentar abgeben	People in Britain like to comment on the weather.	
commercial	Handels-, kaufmännisch, wirtschaftlich	The City is the commercial centre of London where the international banks are.	
commerce	Handel		
convenient	praktisch, bequem	For most older people staying at a hotel is more convenient than camping.	
countryside	Landschaft	The countryside in Ireland is marked by green hills and steep coasts.	= scenery
credit card	Kreditkarte	In the USA credit cards are accepted in almost all shops and restaurants.	

vocabulary	dt. Bedeutung	English sentence	syn/opp
crowded	(mit Menschen) überfüllt	Between 7 and 9 in the morning trains are crowded.	
(to) decide decision	sich entscheiden Entscheidung	We decided to go to England by ferry rather than by plane this time.	
(to) delay	(sich) verspäten, verzögern	Our flight to Majorca was delayed for three hours because of engine problems.	
departure (to) depart	Abreise, Abfahrt abfahren, abreisen	The departure of the train to Glasgow will be at ten past three.	≠ arrival
(to) depend on	abhängen von, abhängig sein von	Many US states – including Florida, Hawaii and Colorado – depend on tourism.	
desert	Wüste	Some southern parts of the Rocky Mountains are as dry as deserts.	
destination	Reiseziel	What is your favourite holiday destination?	
(to) destroy destruction	zerstören, vernichten Zerstörung	Hurricane Katrina destroyed beautiful wooden houses in New Orleans.	
distant distance	fern Entfernung	In Britain the sea never seems very distant. It is only 71 miles to the sea from Birmingham, for example.	= far away
(to) draw	anziehen, ziehen	Disney World Florida draws millions of visitors each year.	= (to) attract
(to) earn	verdienen	A lot of jobs in the tourist sector are badly paid: hotel employees, for example, often earn very little.	

vocabulary	dt. Bedeutung	English sentence	syn/opp
earthquake	*Erdbeben*	In California, earthquakes sometimes shake the ground.	
enjoyable (to) enjoy	*angenehm genießen*	Our stay in Inverness was very enjoyable – we had a really great time there.	= pleasant
enjoyment	*Freude, Vergnügen*	For me, hiking in nature is pure enjoyment.	
entrance (to) enter	*Zugang, Eingang betreten, eintreten*	The entrance to the museum is on the other side of the building.	≠ exit
exchange visit	*Schüleraustausch*	Next year I will take part in an exchange visit to Australia.	
excited exciting excitement	*aufgeregt aufregend Aufregung*	The day before my first flight I was so excited I couldn't sleep half the night.	
excursion	*Ausflug, Exkursion*	While we are in Malta, I'd also like to go on an excursion to the small island of Gozo.	= trip, outing
experience (to) experience	*Erlebnis, Erfahrung erleben*	Seeing the Grand Canyon is an experience you'll never forget.	
famous fame	*berühmt Ruhm*	Las Vegas is famous for its casinos and nightlife.	= well-known
flight (to) fly	*Flug fliegen*	During our flight to New York we ate two meals and we watched a film.	
gift shop	*Geschenkartikelladen*	We stopped at the gift shop to buy some souvenirs.	

vocabulary	dt. Bedeutung	English sentence	syn/opp
guide (to) guide	Reiseführer/-in führen, leiten	On our tour of Hadrian's Wall our guide told us everything about the Romans in Britain.	
guidebook	Reiseführer (Buch)	Reading guidebooks is ideal to learn more about a country's history, culture and main attractions.	= travel guide
(to) hire	mieten	My father hired a boat on the Norfolk Broads for a week last summer.	= (to) rent
holiday job	Ferienarbeit	A lot of pupils take holiday jobs in order to earn a bit of extra money.	
holidaymaker	Urlauber/-in	Most holidaymakers like the food that they get at their hotels.	= vacationer [AE]
holiday resort	Ferienort	Bournemouth is a popular holiday resort on the south coast of England.	
host	Gastgeber/-in	They thanked the host for the wonderful meal.	≠ guest
host family	Gastfamilie	Jenny's host family was really nice – they made her feel like a member of the family.	
(to) inhabit	bewohnen	The people of Trinidad inhabit one of the most beautiful islands in the Caribbean ("Karibik").	= (to) live in
(to) invent invention	erfinden Erfindung	Bungee-jumping was invented in New Zealand.	
journey	Reise	Because of a strike in Calais, we could not continue our journey to England.	= trip

vocabulary	dt. Bedeutung	English sentence	syn/opp
lake	*See*	Loch Ness is a lake in Scotland which may be the home of a "monster".	
landmark	*Wahrzeichen*	Big Ben is one of London's most famous landmarks.	= sight, attraction
lost property office	*Fundbüro*	If you lose your wallet, you should check if someone has handed it in at the lost property office.	= lost-and-found office [AE]
means of transport	*Verkehrsmittel, Beförderungsmittel*	Aeroplanes are still the safest means of transport.	
(to) mind I don't mind	*ausmachen es macht mir nichts aus*	I don't mind staying at home during the holidays.	
(to) miss	*verpassen*	Hardly any tourist who visits London misses a tour of the Tower to see the Crown Jewels.	
national park	*Nationalpark*	Yellowstone and Yosemite are national parks in the USA.	
native	*einheimisch*	Native Americans ("Indianer") have lived in the Grand Canyon region for many centuries.	= indigenous
original origin	*ursprünglich Ursprung, Herkunft*	The bridges in London across the River Thames were originally wooden.	
overseas	*Auslands-, ausländisch*	Overseas visitors are often surprised about American lifestyles.	

vocabulary	dt. Bedeutung	English sentence	syn/opp
package holiday package tour	Pauschalurlaub Pauschalreise	The first foreign package holiday was a tour of Germany organised by Thomas Cook in 1855.	
particularly	besonders, vor allem	Tourism is a particularly important part of the economy.	= especially
passenger	Passagier, Fluggast	The passengers for flight LH4740 were called to gate 62.	
passport	Reisepass	For most trips abroad you need a passport.	
peaceful peace	friedlich Friede	We enjoyed the peaceful atmosphere away from the crowds.	
popular popularity	beliebt Beliebtheit	New York is a popular city for tourists.	≠ unpopular
population (to) populate	Bevölkerung bevölkern	San Francisco has a very large Chinese population.	
(to) protect protection	schützen Schutz	National parks help to protect animals and plants.	
public transport	öffentliche Verkehrmittel	Public transport in London is very expensive.	
reception (to) receive	Empfang empfangen, erhalten	We paid our hotel bill at the reception (desk).	
receptionist	Empfangschef/ Empfangsdame (im Hotel)	Mr Nash worked as a receptionist in Dubai, St Moritz and New York.	
(to) rent	mieten, leihen	In Los Angeles we rented a car to drive around California and Arizona.	= (to) hire
(to) request request	bitten Bitte, Wunsch	Passengers are requested not to leave their luggage unattended.	= (to) ask

vocabulary	dt. Bedeutung	English sentence	syn/opp
reservation **(to) reserve**	*Reservierung* *reservieren*	We had made a reservation because we knew that the hotel would be full in August.	
resort	*Urlaubsort, Ferienort*	Padstow is a beautiful resort by the sea in Cornwall.	
route	*Route, Strecke*	Our route took us along the south-west coast of England.	
rush hour	*Hauptverkehrs-zeit*	If you want to go into the centre of London, try not to travel during the rush hour.	
scenery	*Landschaft*	America's Great West is famous for its beautiful scenery.	= countryside
seaside resort	*Seebad*	Many British families spend their holidays at seaside resorts such as Blackpool, Brighton or Torquay.	
security	*Sicherheit, Sicherheits-*	When you want to fly to the USA you have to go through several security checks at the airport.	= safety
secure	*sicher*		= safe
(to) see	*sehen*	So far nobody has seen a monster in Loch Ness.	
serious	*ernst, ernsthaft*	America's big cities have serious problems with traffic and crime.	
shopping trip	*Einkaufstour*	Alan and Rita are going on a shopping trip to France.	

vocabulary	dt. Bedeutung	English sentence	syn/opp
sight	Sehenswürdigkeit	Golden Gate Bridge is one of the well-known sights of San Francisco.	= landmark, attraction
sightseeing (to) go sight-seeing	Besichtigung(en) auf Besichti-gungstour gehen	We did our sightseeing tour of Edinburgh on an open double-decker bus.	
single room	Einzelzimmer	As Steve was travelling on his own, he booked a single room.	
site	Ort, Platz	The house stands on the site of an old Roman camp.	
(to) spend	verbringen	The Youngs always spend their summer holidays in the Canary Islands.	
(to) take off	starten	You should arrive at the airport two hours before your plane takes off.	
term	Ausdruck	The term "Celtic Fringe" refers to countries in which Celtic languages are still spoken (e. g. Wales, Scotland and Ireland).	= name
tour	Rundreise, Tour	Harriet is planning a bike tour of the Lake District.	
tourism	Tourismus	A lot of San Francisco's money comes from banking and tourism.	
tourist attraction	Sehenswürdig-keit, Touristen-attraktion	The Empire State building is one of the many tourist attractions in New York.	
tourist information	Fremden-verkehrsamt	If you are looking for a place to stay, it's best to ask at the tourist informa-tion.	= tourist office

vocabulary	dt. Bedeutung	English sentence	syn/opp
tour operator	*Reiseveranstalter*	Some tour operators offer bungee jumping from Victoria Falls Bridge.	
traveller (to) travel	*Reisende(r) reisen*	Travellers can get to England by plane, ferry or through the Channel Tunnel.	
travel agent	*Reiseberater/-in*	The travel agent worked out the prices for a caravan holiday in Ireland.	
travel agent's	*Reisebüro*	I went to the travel agent's to pick up brochures about holidays in Wales.	= travel agency
valley	*Tal*	I would like to see the Valley of the Kings in Egypt.	
(to) vary varied variety	*variieren, wechseln, schwanken vielfältig Vielfalt*	The climate in Canada varies from region to region.	
youth hostel	*Jugendherberge*	Youth hostels offer relatively cheap accommodation for young people.	

Family

vocabulary	dt. Bedeutung	English sentence	syn/opp
(to) adopt	adoptieren, die Patenschaft übernehmen	Some couples who can't have their own children decide to adopt a child.	
adoption	Adoption		
adult	Erwachsene(r)	Teenagers often have the feeling that adults don't understand them at all.	= grown-up ≠ youngster, child
ancestor	Vorfahr(e)/ Vorfahrin	Shail is British but his ancestors came from India.	≠ descendant
aunt	Tante	Aunt Mary is my dad's sister.	
birth	Geburt		
(to) give birth	zur Welt bringen	Sarah gave birth to her second child at 29.	= (to) bear a child
birthday	Geburtstag	When is your birthday?	
(to) bring up	großziehen, erziehen	When his parents died, Marc was brought up by his grandfather.	= (to) raise
care	Sorge, Sorgfalt		
(to) care for	sich kümmern um	Caring for children is a very responsible task.	= (to) look after
(to) take care of	sich kümmern um, Sorge tragen für	Today, more fathers stay at home to take care of their children.	
careful	sorgfältig, vorsichtig		
childhood	Kindheit	Some people say that their childhood was the happiest time of their lives.	
couple	(Ehe-)Paar	Meg and Andy are so in love – they make a really great couple.	

vocabulary	dt. Bedeutung	English sentence	syn/opp
cousin	Cousin/Cousine	That's my cousin Joe – he's Aunt Mary's son.	
date of birth	Geburtsdatum	Amelia's date of birth is January 3, 2001.	
divorce	Scheidung	Jane decided to get a divorce from Adam.	≠ marriage
divorced	geschieden	Alan's parents are divorced.	≠ married
familiar	vertraut	Then, suddenly, I heard a loud, familiar voice.	= well-known ≠ unfamiliar
family member	Familienmitglied, Angehörige(r)	At my grandmother's birthday all the family members came together.	
female	weiblich	The number of female engineers has increased.	≠ male
foster child	Pflegekind	A foster child is taken care of by a couple who are not his/her natural parents.	
grandchild/ -son/ -daughter	Enkel/-in	Mr Reeves likes playing with his grandchildren.	
grandparents	Großeltern	When I can't get what I want from my mum, I always ask my grandparents.	
household	Haushalt	Nearly all households have internet access today.	
housework (to) do house-work	Hausarbeit Hausarbeit machen	A lot of people don't really enjoy doing housework, such as washing the dishes.	
human being	Mensch	All human beings should enjoy the same rights.	= man
husband	Ehemann	Mr Miller is Mrs Miller's husband.	≠ wife
individual	individuell, persönlich	Everybody has their indivi-dual likes and dislikes.	≠ general, common

vocabulary	dt. Bedeutung	English sentence	syn/opp
marriage	*Heirat, Ehe*	My parents look back on 20 years of marriage.	≠ divorce
(to) marry	*heiraten*	Amy said she would only marry for love, not for money.	≠ (to) divorce
member	*Mitglied*	At my grandfather's birthday all members of the family came together.	
membership	*Mitgliedschaft*	The membership of our football club is going down.	
neighbour	*Nachbar/-in*	We often help our neighbours and they help us.	
neighbourhood	*Nachbarschaft, Viertel*	We live in a quiet neighbourhood.	
nephew	*Neffe*	Harry is the son of my elder sister Jane. He is my nephew.	
niece	*Nichte*	Carly is the daughter of my younger brother Tom. She is my niece.	
orphan	*Waise(-nkind)*	Oliver lost his parents as a baby and grew up as an orphan.	
parental leave	*Elternzeit*	Simon took parental leave when his wife started to work again.	= family leave
patchwork family	*Familie, in der Kinder von verschiedenen Eltern aufwachsen*	The number of patchwork families is increasing.	
place of birth	*Geburtsort*	A passport shows your name and place of birth.	
pregnancy	*Schwangerschaft*	There has been an increase in teenage pregnancies.	
(to be/become/ get) pregnant	*schwanger (sein/werden)*	Mrs Miller is pregnant with her second child.	

vocabulary	dt. Bedeutung	English sentence	syn/opp
(to) raise	*großziehen, aufziehen*	Mrs Muir raised her three children alone.	= (to) bring up
relative	*Verwandte(r)*	My uncle Jimmy is my favourite relative.	
same-sex marriage	*gleichgeschlecht-liche Ehe*	A law to allow same-sex marriage in England was passed in 2013.	= gay marriage
(to) separate	*sich trennen*	After 15 years of marriage Ben's parents separated.	
single	*ledig*	Today, most people do not marry young; they remain single longer.	≠ married
single parent, single mother/father	*Alleinerziehen-de(r), allein erziehende(r) Mutter/Vater*	A single parent is a mother or father who looks after her/his child or children without a partner.	
(to) start a family	*eine Familie gründen*	Jane and Leo started a family when they were still teenagers.	
(to) support a family	*eine Familie ernähren*	If you earn money you can support a family.	
twin	*Zwilling*	The Carlyn twins look very much alike.	
wedding	*Hochzeit*	Jack and Ava's wedding was really romantic.	
wife	*Ehefrau*	Pete met his wife Karin when he worked in Africa.	≠ husband
youngster	*Jugendliche(r)*	David Attenborough became interested in animals as a youngster.	= teenager, child
youth	*Jugendliche(r)*	Most youths love listening to their favourite music.	≠ adult

School

vocabulary	dt. Bedeutung	English sentence	syn/opp
assembly	Versammlung	In England school starts with assembly at 9 o'clock every morning.	
(to) assemble	sich versammeln	All school children assemble in the auditorium.	= (to) come together, (to) meet
assignment	Aufgabe, Hausaufgabe	Read all the assignments first before you start on your answers.	= task, exercise, homework
at school	in der Schule	Did you have a good day at school?	
(to) attend school	die Schule besuchen	Most pupils in the UK attend state schools.	= (to) go to school
basic skill	Grundfertigkeit	Reading, writing and arithmetic – the "three Rs" – are basic skills.	
(to) be good at	gut sein in	Eric is very good at sport – he is our best footballer.	≠ (to) be bad/weak at
boarding school	Internat	At the age of 8 Prince William was sent to a boarding school.	
(to) bully	mobben, schikanieren	Bullying can make life at school very difficult for boys and girls.	= (to) intimidate
bullying	Mobbing, Schikanieren		
bully	gemeine(r) Mitschüler/-in	Barry was one of the worst bullies at my school.	
certificate	Urkunde	My certificate shows that I took exams in English, Maths and German.	

vocabulary	dt. Bedeutung	English sentence	syn/opp
charge (to be) in charge of	*Verantwortung verantwortlich (sein) für*	A headmaster or head-mistress is in charge of a school.	
(to) cheat	*schummeln, betrügen*	It never pays to cheat at school.	
chemistry	*Chemie*	My uncle is a professor of chemistry at the University of Bristol.	
(to) choose choice	*wählen Auswahl*	In the USA pupils can choose some of their school subjects.	
classmate	*Klassen-kamerad/-in*	Simon always helps his classmates with their homework.	= schoolmate
composition	*Aufsatz*	I wrote a composition about my visit to Disney World in Orlando, Florida.	= essay
comprehensive school	*Gesamtschule*	Lily attends a big compre-hensive school with over two thousand pupils.	
compulsory	*obligatorisch, verpflichtend*	Education in Britain is compulsory for all children between 5 and 16.	= obligatory ≠ voluntary
(to) copy	*abschreiben, kopieren*	Use your own words in your answers. Do not copy from the text.	
(to) correct correction	*korrigieren Korrektur*	A lot of teachers say they spend more time correct-ing than teaching.	= (to) mark
curriculum	*Lehrplan*	The curriculum lays down which subjects and skills pupils should be taught.	
day out	*(Tages-)Ausflug*	Last Tuesday we had a day out at the zoo in Regent's Park.	= school trip, excursion

vocabulary	dt. Bedeutung	English sentence	syn/opp
(to) do one's homework	*Hausaufgaben machen*	Simon always does his homework straight after school.	
(to) do well	*gut abschneiden*	Students work hard to do well in their exams.	
domestic science	*Hauswirtschafts-lehre, -kunde*	In domestic science students learn how to cook.	
drama group	*Theatergruppe, Theatertruppe*	Noah loves acting – he is a member of the school drama group.	
(to) drop out of school	*die Schule abbrechen / vorzeitig verlassen*	Jake dropped out of school and started working at a supermarket.	
education	*Ausbildung, Bildung*	Parents want their children to have a good education.	
(to) educate	*erziehen, ausbilden*	My aunt is really educated – she knows all about art, history and science.	
educated	*gebildet*		
effect	*Wirkung, Auswirkung*	Pupils know that exams have a big effect on their future.	
(to) enter	*eintreten*	In 1995 Prince William entered the exclusive Eton College.	
	teilnehmen an	Jessica entered a competition in creative writing.	
entrance	*Eingang, Eintritt*		
entrance examination	*Aufnahmeprü-fung, Zulassungs-test*	The entrance examination to Arts College is very difficult.	= admission test
essay	*Aufsatz*	Jane had to write an essay on George Washington.	= composition
exam	*Prüfung*	May, June and July are the main months for exams at English schools.	= test

vocabulary	dt. Bedeutung	English sentence	syn/opp
exchange programme	*Austausch-programm*	Every year hundreds of young people from all over Europe take part in an exchange programme and spend a year in the USA.	
excursion (to) go on an excursion	*Ausflug einen Ausflug machen*	The class went on an excursion to Buckingham Palace.	= school trip
exercise book	*Heft*	Open your exercise books, please.	
extra classes	*Nachhilfe*	Ryan has extra classes in maths and physics.	
(to) fail	*nicht bestehen, durchfallen*	If an American student fails a number of subjects, he/she usually does not have to stay at school for an extra year.	≠ (to) pass
failure	*Versagen, Misserfolg*	The last project we did was a total failure but our next one will be better.	≠ success
(to) finish school	*die Schule beenden*	As soon as I finish school I want to work and earn some money.	≠ (to) start school
foreign language	*Fremdsprache*	Foreign languages are becoming more and more important.	≠ native language, mother tongue
form teacher	*Klassenlehrer/-in*	Mr Finlay is our new form teacher.	
GCSE (= General Certificate of Secondary Education)	*Schulabschluss (entspricht in etwa dem deutschen Realschulabschluss)*	English pupils take their GCSE exams at the age of about 16.	

vocabulary	dt. Bedeutung	English sentence	syn/opp
graduate (to) graduate	Absolvent/-in, Abgänger/-in die Abschluss-prüfung bestehen, abgehen von	University graduates generally have a better chance of finding a good job.	
grammar school	Gymnasium	Most children in England go to comprehensive schools. However, there might be a revival of grammar schools.	
(to) hate	hassen	I always liked school, but my sister hated it.	≠ (to) love
hate	Hass	Hate is a very negative emotion.	= hatred ≠ love
headmaster headmistress	Schulleiter, Direktor Schulleiterin, Direktorin	The new headmaster was strictly against using smart-phones at school.	= principal [AE]
high school [AE]	weiterführende Schule, High-school	After high school, Mason wants to go to Berkeley University in California.	
(to) improve improvement	(sich) verbessern, besser werden Verbesserung	My English has improved a lot since I spent a year in Britain.	≠ (to) get worse
infant school [BE]	Vorschule, Spielschule	Children between 4 and 7 years of age go to infant schools.	= elementary school [AE]
(to) interrupt	unterbrechen	Noisy kids often interrupt the lessons.	
language course	Sprachkurs	In my holidays I want to attend a language course.	
(to) leave	verlassen	Steve left school and worked in a fast food restaurant.	

vocabulary	dt. Bedeutung	English sentence	syn/opp
lesson	*Unterrichts-stunde, Lektion*	Every Tuesday we have two English lessons.	
library	*Bücherei, Bibliothek*	There aren't many books in our school library.	
(to) mark	*benoten, bewerten, korrigieren*	Our maths teacher says he has too many papers to mark.	
mark	*Schulnote*	Phoebe is working hard to get better marks in English and French.	= grade [AE]
maths	*Mathe*	Hannah is very good at maths.	
meeting	*Versammlung, Besprechung, Treffen*	The meeting between parents and teachers began shortly after six.	
native language	*Muttersprache*	Many people in Florida speak Spanish as their native language.	= mother tongue ≠ foreign language
native speaker	*Mutter-sprachler/-in*	The Chinese language (Mandarin) has the highest number of native speakers.	
numeracy	*Rechnen*	Numeracy is one of the most important skills for young children to learn.	
oral	*mündlich*	I hate oral exams. I just get too nervous.	≠ written
(to) pass an exam	*eine Prüfung bestehen*	All my classmates hope that we will pass our final exams next summer.	≠ (to) fail an exam
PE (= Physical Education)	*Sportunterricht*	Most parents and teachers think that physical education is important.	= sport

vocabulary	dt. Bedeutung	English sentence	syn/opp
pen friend	Brieffreund/-in	My French pen friend Michelle will come and visit me next summer.	
performance	Leistung	Jayden trains hard every week, but he is not happy with his performance.	= achievement
	Vorstellung, Aufführung	The performances of our school drama group are always good.	= show
physics	Physik	Many pupils find physics too abstract.	
(to) praise	loben	The head teacher praised Tim and Christina for their work on the school magazine.	≠ (to) tell s.o. off
(to) prepare	sich vorbereiten	Pupils have to prepare for exams by reading a lot.	= (to) get ready
pressure (to) put pressure on	Druck Druck ausüben auf	Exam pressure is a problem for many pupils.	= stress
primary school	Grundschule	After primary school English children go to a secondary school.	
public school [BE]	Privatschule	Eton, Harrow, Winchester, Westminster and Rugby are famous English public schools.	= private/ independent school ≠ state school
(to) punish	(be-)strafen	Schools try to punish bullies harder.	≠ (to) praise
punishment	Strafe	As a punishment, bullies could be excluded from school trips, for example.	
pupil	Schüler/-in	The number of pupils at private schools is rising.	= student

vocabulary	dt. Bedeutung	English sentence	syn/opp
qualification (to) qualify qualified	*Qualifikation, Abschlusszeugnis* *sich qualifizieren* *ausgebildet, qualifiziert*	What qualifications and skills are needed for this job? My brother Ethan is a qualified nurse.	= skilled ≠ unskilled
relationship	*Beziehung*	School trips help pupils to develop a better relationship with each other.	
(to) repeat	*wiederholen*	In Germany pupils who get bad results in their tests have to repeat a year.	
scared	*verängstigt*	Most kids are a bit scared when they start school.	= frightened
school fees	*Schulgeld, Schulgebühren*	At private schools pupils have to pay school fees of £10,000 a year or more.	
school holiday(s) [BE]	*Schulferien*	In my last school holidays I visited my aunt in Glasgow.	= vacation [AE]
school leaver	*Schulabgänger/-in*	Young school leavers often turn to the careers officer for advice.	
school meal	*(Mittag-)Essen in der Schule*	Holly's favourite school meal is fish and chips.	= school lunch, school dinner
school trip	*Schulfahrt, Klassenreise*	Many parents say that school trips are too expensive.	= excursion
school uniform	*Schuluniform*	At British schools pupils wear school uniforms.	
school yard	*Schulhof*	Some pupils play football in the school yard during the breaks.	
school-leaving certificate	*Abgangszeugnis*	At 16 some German pupils receive their school-leaving certificate.	

vocabulary	dt. Bedeutung	English sentence	syn/opp
secondary school [BE]	*weiterführende Schule*	Joe was the first in his family to finish secondary school and go to university.	= high school [AE]
(to) sit a paper	*eine Klausur schreiben*	We had to sit a paper on the Glorious Revolution of 1688.	= (to) do a test
skill	*Fähigkeit, Fertigkeit*	At school young people learn lots of skills which will be useful for them in their jobs later on.	
skilled	*ausgebildet, qualifiziert*	Many companies are looking for skilled workers.	≠ unskilled
(to) spell	*(richtig) schreiben, buchstabieren*	How do you spell this word, please?	
spelling	*Rechtschreib-; Rechtschreibung*	There were too many spelling mistakes in Tom's essay.	
state school	*staatliche Schule*	State schools are free for all children.	≠ public school [BE]
(to) stay on	*länger in der Schule bleiben*	When they are 16 English pupils can leave school. Some stay on to take their A-levels.	≠ (to) drop out of
(to) study	*studieren*	Prince William studied Geography in Scotland.	
subject	*Schulfach*	Jenny's favourite subjects are PE and history.	
(to) take an exam	*eine Prüfung machen*	All British school children take exams when they are 16.	
talent	*Begabung*	Daniel has creative talent. He wants to be an artist.	= gift
talented	*begabt*	Mia is really talented.	= gifted

vocabulary	dt. Bedeutung	English sentence	syn/opp
term	*Trimester*	In England the school year has three terms: spring, summer and winter term.	
textbook	*Lehrbuch*	Unit 1 of our textbook is about Australia.	
training	*Ausbildung*	In England, many school leavers start a job without any training.	
training course	*Ausbildungskurs*	Various organisations offer training courses for school leavers who do not have a job.	
university	*Universität*	After school Charlotte wants to go to Oxford University.	
vocabulary	*Wortschatz, Vokabular*	We have to take a vocabulary test every week.	
(to) worry	*sich sorgen*	Zoe worried about the result of her last English test.	
written test	*Klassenarbeit, schriftliche Arbeit*	I don't think I did very well in the last written test in physics.	≠ oral exam

Leisure

vocabulary	dt. Bedeutung	English sentence	syn/opp
activity	Beschäftigung, Aktivität	Ruby's favourite activity after school is cycling.	
adventure	Abenteuer	A helicopter flight over the Grand Canyon is quite an adventure.	
amusement	Spaß, Unter-haltung	She listened to his jokes with amusement.	
amusing	unterhaltsam	This novel is really amusing – you should read it!	= enjoyable, pleasant
athletics	Leichtathletik	She won the athletics on Sports Day.	
(to) do athletics	Leichtathletik betreiben	Max has been doing athletics since he was twelve.	
audience	Publikum, Zuschauer	An international audience listened to the concerts at the Royal Albert Hall.	
(to) avoid	vermeiden	If you want to avoid mass tourism, go to the west coast of Majorca.	
(to) celebrate	feiern	St. Patrick's Day is cele-brated on March 17.	
celebration	Feier, Fest		
(to) cycle	Fahrrad fahren		= (to) ride a bike
cycling	Radfahren, Radsport	The Tour de France is the world's most important cycling event.	
(to) decide	entscheiden	As it was raining, we de-cided to go to the mu-seum.	
decision	Entscheidung	It was a good decision to stay out of the rain.	

vocabulary	dt. Bedeutung	English sentence	syn/opp
(to) entertain entertainment	unterhalten Unterhaltung	The best TV programmes entertain you and educate you at the same time.	
event	Ereignis	Wimbledon is an important sports event in the United Kingdom.	
exercise (to) exercise	(körperliche) Bewegung, Training trainieren, üben	The doctor told Sandra to do more exercise. Exercising just ten minutes a day can improve your health.	 = (to) train
(to) explore exploration	erkunden, erforschen Erforschung	We explored the area around Loch Ness on bikes – but we didn't see the monster.	
fair	Messe, Markt, Jahrmarkt	We spent the day looking through books at the book fair.	
fashion fashion magazine	Mode Modezeitschrift	Fashions come and go. Chloe's mother often buys fashion magazines such as Vogue or Elle.	
fashionable	modisch	Leo was wearing fashionable shoes.	
favourite	Lieblings-	Reading is my favourite hobby.	
festival	Festspiel, Festival	The Edinburgh Festival takes place in August and September.	
(to) get away	entfliehen, entkommen	We always try to get away from the crowds – we prefer quieter places.	= (to) escape
(to) go (window) shopping	einen (Schaufenster-)Bummel machen	My aunts Mary and Mable always go window shopping at the weekend.	

vocabulary	dt. Bedeutung	English sentence	syn/opp
(to) go for a walk	*einen Spaziergang machen*	Would you like to go for a walk to get some fresh air?	
gymnastics	*Turnen*	In gymnastics some world record holders are still at school.	
indoor	*Hallen-*	Our hotel had a very nice indoor pool.	≠ outdoor
indoors	*drinnen*	On cold days we stayed indoors.	≠ outdoors
(to) be interested in **interest**	*sich interessieren für* *Interesse*	My parents are very much interested in music – they often go to concerts.	
(to) keep fit	*fit, gesund bleiben*	My neighbour does aerobics three times a week to keep fit.	
latest	*neueste(r/s)*	Victoria is always dressed in the latest fashion.	
leisure (time)	*Freizeit*	What do you like to do in your leisure time?	= spare time, free time
leisure centre	*Freizeitzentrum*	Moray Leisure Centre has a pool, a health centre and a coffee bar.	
(to) listen to music / to the radio	*Musik/Radio hören*	Ken's favourite pastime is listening to music – he loves heavy metal.	
(to) look forward to	*sich freuen auf*	Michael is looking forward to going hiking at the weekend.	
musician	*Musiker/-in*	A world-famous musician will give a concert in our town next Saturday.	
outdoor	*Außen-, im Freien*	The holiday camp offers a lot of outdoor activities.	≠ indoor
outdoors	*draußen, im Freien*	I enjoy being outdoors and getting fresh air.	≠ indoors

vocabulary	dt. Bedeutung	English sentence	syn/opp
(to) paint	*malen*	Dave is very good at painting – his pictures are really nice!	
pastime	*Zeitvertreib*	Playing video games is Alexander's favourite pastime.	
(to) perform **performance**	*aufführen* *Aufführung*	The drama group will perform their next play at our school in May.	= (to) stage
(to) phone	*anrufen*	Lisa phoned her friends to invite them to her party.	= (to) call
(to) play a musical instrument	*ein Musikinstrument spielen*	I was ten when I started playing an instrument.	
(to) play chess	*Schach spielen*	Do you think that people who play chess are more intelligent?	
(to) play in a band	*in einer Band spielen*	Have you ever played in a school band?	
(to) play on the computer	*am Computer spielen*	Bob's mother thinks that her son spends too much time playing on his computer.	
popular **popularity**	*beliebt* *Beliebtheit*	Watching television is a popular pastime.	≠ unpopular
(to) relax	*sich entspannen*	The passengers could relax and watch a film during the long flight.	
(to) ride a bike	*Fahrrad fahren*	Riding a bike is much healthier than going by car.	= (to) cycle
(to) set out	*aufbrechen*	We set out on our tour at 4 o'clock in the morning.	
sight	*Sehenswürdigkeit*	London has many interesting sights.	

vocabulary	dt. Bedeutung	English sentence	syn/opp
sightseeing **(to) go sight-seeing**	*Besichtigungen* *auf Besichti-gungstour gehen*	During the sightseeing tour our guide told us all about the Great Fire of London (1666).	
spare time	*Freizeit*	Some managers cannot relax in their spare time.	= leisure, free time
spare-time activity	*Freizeitbeschäf-tigung*	For many young people sport is their most impor-tant spare-time activity.	
spectacular	*atemberaubend, fantastisch*	In Disney's Epcot Center you can watch a spectacu-lar laser show.	
stay	*Aufenthalt*	"Enjoy your stay," said the hotel manager.	
(to) stay at a hotel	*in einem Hotel wohnen*	Staying at a hotel is more expensive than camping.	
(to) surf the internet	*im Internet surfen*	My brother always spends hours surfing the internet.	
(to) take a break	*eine Pause machen*	On our bike tour we took a break by the riverside.	
(to) take part in	*teilnehmen an*	All pupils wanted to take part in the school trip to Cardiff.	
(to) take place	*stattfinden*	In England, horse races take place at Newmarket, Epsom, Cheltenham and Aintree, for example.	
tourist attraction	*Touristen-attraktion*	Disneyland in Florida offers many tourist attractions.	
trainers [BE]	*Turnschuhe*	In 1979 Nike produced the first trainers with air in their soles.	= sneakers [AE]
trendy **trend**	*modisch* *Trend, Richtung*	It used to be very trendy to wear a coloured plastic band on your wrist.	

vocabulary	dt. Bedeutung	English sentence	syn/opp
vacation [AE]	*Ferien*	Where are you going for your vacation?	= holiday [BE]
viewer	*Zuschauer/-in*	The Super Bowl attracts more viewers than any other TV event.	
(to) watch sport on TV	*Sport im Fern- sehen sehen*	Luke shouldn't just watch sport on TV – he should go out and do it.	
(to) watch television	*fernsehen*	Watching television for hours every day can be bad for your health.	
(to) wear	*(Kleidung) tragen*	In the 1950s and '60s women were not allowed to wear trousers in banks or offices.	
youth centre/club	*Jugendzentrum, -klub*	The mayor promised that the city would build a new youth centre.	

Sport

vocabulary	dt. Bedeutung	English sentence	syn/opp
ability	Fähigkeit	In games people test their own ability against that of others.	= skill, talent ≠ inability
(to) be able	fähig sein, können		
abroad	ins, im Ausland	Our team played abroad for the first time this year.	= overseas ≠ at home
achievement (to) achieve	Leistung erreichen, leisten	Some politicians think that athletes' achievements show the success of a nation.	
activity	Beschäftigung, Aktivität	In the summer Megan and Jennifer like to do outdoor activities, such as canoeing and hiking.	≠ inactivity
(to) act action active	handeln Handlung aktiv, lebhaft		
(to) admire admiration	bewundern Bewunderung	Who do you admire most: a pop star, a writer, a film star or an athlete?	≠ (to) scorn
(to) adopt adoption	übernehmen, annehmen Übernahme	Cricket was adopted by many English-speaking countries around the world.	
aerobics (to) do aerobics	Aerobic Aerobic machen	My neighbour does aerobics three times a week to keep fit.	
against	gegen	Our next match will be against the current champions.	= versus
amateur	Amateur/-in	Amateurs practise their sport without receiving any money.	≠ professional, pro
angry anger	zornig, wütend Zorn, Ärger, Wut	The fans are angry because the best player is going to join another club.	= furious, mad ≠ pleased

vocabulary	dt. Bedeutung	English sentence	syn/opp
arrow	*Pfeil*	In archery ("Bogenschie-ßen") they use bows and arrows.	
(to) association	*Verband*	The English Football Association (FA) was created in 1863.	
(to) assume	*glauben, annehmen*	The fans assume that their club will win the league again this year.	= (to) suppose, (to) believe
(to) assure	*versichern, zusichern, beteuern*	The player assured the referee that he had not touched the ball with his hands.	= (to) make sth. sure or certain
athlete	*Athlet/-in*	The aim of any excellent athlete is to take part in the Olympic Games.	= sportsman, sportswoman
athletics	*Leichtathletik*	British children can do athletics at school.	
attack **(to) attack**	*Angriff* *angreifen*	The trainer said, "Attack is the best form of defence."	≠ defence
(to) attend	*besuchen, anwesend sein*	More than 95,000 people attended the final.	= (to) be present at
audience	*Zuschauer, Publikum*	Boxing always attracts a large TV audience.	
awful	*schrecklich*	After fouling his friend Jim, Harry felt awful.	= terrible
(to) behave	*sich benehmen*	"Some youngsters just cannot behave on the sports ground," the old man said.	
(to) bet	*wetten*	The British like betting on horses and dogs.	
boring	*langweilig*	Most people find fencing ("Fechten") boring but I like it.	

vocabulary	dt. Bedeutung	English sentence	syn/opp
box office	Kasse	The box office will open at 6 o'clock.	
business	Geschäft	In the USA basketball is big business.	
(to) challenge challenge	herausfordern Herausforderung	The young boxer will challenge the title holder.	
champion championship	Sieger/-in, Champion Meisterschaft	Manchester United have won the title of English football champion many times.	
(to) cheer	anfeuern	The spectators cheer their team.	
competition (to) compete competitive	Wettbewerb konkurrieren konkurrenzfähig	There is strong competition in professional sport.	
crowd	Menge	When David scored in the last minute the crowd went wild.	
defeat	Niederlage	The fans were very sad about the defeat of their team.	≠ victory, triumph
(to) defend defence defensive	verteidigen Verteidigung defensiv	The boxer successfully defended his title against the newcomer.	
(to) deserve	verdienen	Our team are playing very well today; I think they deserve to win.	
(to) do sport	Sport treiben	You should do more sport to keep fit.	
doping	Doping	Doping is a massive problem in professional sports.	
draw	Unentschieden	Our last three matches ended in a draw.	

vocabulary	dt. Bedeutung	English sentence	syn/opp
effort	*Anstrengung*	If you practise hard, your efforts will be rewarded.	
entertainment (to) entertain	*Unterhaltung unterhalten*	Sport has become a part of the entertainment industry.	
equipment (to) equip	*Ausrüstung ausstatten*	Excellent athletes usually get their equipment free from sponsors.	
(to) exercise	*trainieren, üben*	You will get better if you exercise regularly.	= (to) train
fight (to) fight	*Kampf kämpfen*	In boxing, many fights are decided on points.	
final	*Endspiel*	If we win our next match, we'll reach the final.	
(to) gain	*erlangen, gewinnen*	Who do you think will gain the title of "Sportsman/ Sportswoman of the Year"?	= (to) win
(to) get rid of	*loswerden*	Some people get rid of their aggression in sport.	
goalkeeper	*Torwart/-in, Torhüter/-in*	Our team has the best goalkeeper of the second division.	= goalie [colloquial]
ground	*Stadion*	Chelsea FC's home ground is Stamford Bridge.	= stadium
healthy	*gesund*	Sport keeps your body fit and healthy.	≠ unhealthy
health	*Gesundheit*	Regular exercise is good for your health.	≠ illness
hooligan	*Rowdy, Hooligan*	Young hooligans caused trouble at the matches.	
hooliganism	*Rowdytum*	How can we prevent football hooliganism?	
(to) injure injury	*verletzen Verletzung*	Our best player is out for this season because he has injured his knee.	= (to) hurt

vocabulary	dt. Bedeutung	English sentence	syn/opp
(to) last	dauern	A game of cricket lasts all day.	
manager	Trainer/-in	The manager decided to buy a new goalkeeper from abroad.	= trainer, coach
match	Spiel	"Match of the Day" is a popular programme on British television.	= game
muscle	Muskel	In swimming you use more muscles in the body than in any other form of exercise.	
Olympic Games	Olympische Spiele	The motto of the Olympic Games is: Faster, Higher, Stronger.	
penalty	Elfmeter, Strafstoß	He scored the penalty which decided the game.	
physical	körperlich	You have to do more physical exercise or you will get too fat!	≠ mental
pitch	Spielfeld	Some fans threw beer cans onto the pitch.	= field, sports ground
pleasure	Vergnügen	Very often the pleasure of sport gets lost when too much money is involved.	= joy, enjoyment, delight
(to) please pleasant	gefallen angenehm		
popular	beliebt	Football is the most popular sport in England.	= well-liked ≠ unpopular
popularity	Beliebtheit	The popularity of women's football is increasing.	
power	Kraft, Stärke; Macht	The cheerleaders chanted, "We got power, we got style!"	= strength ≠ weakness
powerful	stark; mächtig		
prestige	Ansehen	As soon as the question of prestige arises, fair play disappears.	= status

vocabulary	dt. Bedeutung	English sentence	syn/opp
professional	*Profi-, Berufs- (sportler/-in)*	A professional football player can earn a lot of money in a couple of years.	≠ amateur
record	*Rekord*	Jenny set up a new record in the swimming competition.	
referee	*Schiedsrichter/-in*	The referee stopped the match, because the players started to fight each other.	
reputation	*Ruf*	Because of the hooligans Britain's football fans have a bad reputation.	
riot	*(Straßen-) Schlacht*	There are often riots in the streets on the way to the stadium.	
rival	*Konkurrent/-in*	Arsenal and Manchester United are rivals.	= competitor ≠ partner
rule	*Bestimmung, Verbot, Vorschrift*	Games are played according to rules.	
(to) score a goal/point	*ein Tor schießen; einen Punkt erzielen*	I have scored some goals! Ava scored six points for her team.	
(to) shout	*schreien*	The fans shouted, "Our team will win!"	= (to) scream
(to) sign a contract	*einen Vertrag unterschreiben*	The basketball star signed a million-dollar contract with a new sponsor.	
soccer [AE]	*(europäischer) Fußball*	European football can also be called "soccer".	= football [BE]
spectator	*Zuschauer/-in*	The spectators went wild when their club won the championship.	

vocabulary	dt. Bedeutung	English sentence	syn/opp
sports event	*Sportveran-staltung*	People go to watch sports events because they find them exciting.	
sportsman sportswoman	*Sportler Sportlerin*	For a good sportsman or sportswoman it is also important to be fair.	= athlete
stimulant	*Aufputschmittel*	Sometimes athletes take stimulants to win.	= drug
success (to) succeed successful	*Erfolg Erfolg haben erfolgreich*	Success is a must for pro-fessional football clubs.	
supporter	*Anhänger/-in, Fan*	I've always been a keen supporter of our local team.	= fan
tournament	*Turnier*	Wimbledon is the biggest tennis tournament in Britain.	
track	*(Renn-)Bahn*	Monte Carlo and Monza are famous tracks for Formula 1 races.	= race track
(to) train trainer training	*trainieren Trainer Training*	Top athletes have to train very hard every day.	
(to) vandalise vandalism	*zerstören Zerstörungswut*	On their way home from the match, some hooligans vandalised trains and buses.	= (to) destroy
victory victorious	*Sieg siegreich*	The team celebrated their victory with the fans.	≠ defeat
whistle (to) whistle	*Pfeife pfeifen*	The referee blew his whistle to stop the game.	
world championship	*Weltmeister-schaft*	Germany won the football world championship in 2014.	= world cup

Health

vocabulary	dt. Bedeutung	English sentence	syn/opp
addicted addiction	süchtig Sucht	Many people become addicted to alcohol.	
(to) admit	zugeben, zugestehen	Brian admitted that he had drunk too much.	≠ (to) deny
(to) affect	sich auswirken auf, betreffen	Alcohol affects clear thinking and causes accidents.	
(to) arrest	festnehmen, verhaften	A 25-year-old man was arrested for selling drugs.	≠ (to) set free
available	verfügbar	The patient wanted to know what treatments are available for the disease.	
average on average	durchschnittlich, Durchschnitts-, im Durchschnitt	An average man needs about 2,500 calories a day.	
balanced diet	ausgewogene Ernährung	If you want to stay healthy, you should eat a balanced diet.	≠ imbalanced diet
(to) ban ban	verbieten Verbot	Cigarettes are banned in public buildings.	≠ (to) allow
beef	Rindfleisch	Hindus are not allowed to eat beef. They believe cows are sacred.	
(to) blame	die Schuld geben, Vorwürfe machen	Doctors blame sugary foods for the weight problems many children have.	
(to) boil	kochen, zum Kochen bringen	Some of my school friends like cooking, while others cannot even boil an egg.	
(to be/feel) bored boredom	gelangweilt (sein) Langeweile	Some teenagers eat too much because they feel bored.	≠ thrilled, excited

vocabulary	dt. Bedeutung	English sentence	syn/opp
brain	*Gehirn*	Too much alcohol damages the brain and many other parts of the body.	
busy	*belebt, geschäftig*	Pubs are very busy at lunchtime.	
calorie	*Kalorie*	A large coke has 226 calories.	
cancer	*Krebs*	Smoking can cause lung cancer.	
(to) cause	*verursachen*	Drugs and alcohol cause a lot of problems in families.	
cereal	*Frühstückszerealien (Cornflakes, Müsli)*	I have cereal for breakfast every day.	
chain	*Kette*	Fast food chains are trying to improve their image.	
(to) check	*überprüfen, kontrollieren*	The police check pubs to make sure they are not selling alcohol to under-18s.	= (to) control
(to) complain complaint	*sich beklagen, sich beschweren Beschwerde*	My grandma complains that she cannot walk fast anymore.	
(to) connect connection	*verbinden Verbindung*	Teenagers often connect alcohol with the attractive things in life.	= (to) link, (to) combine
(to) contain contents	*enthalten Inhalt*	Soft drinks contain a lot of sugar and can make you fat.	
(to) cook cooking	*kochen, eine Mahlzeit zubereiten Essen, Mahlzeiten, Küche*	Everybody should be able to cook a proper, healthy meal. Many tourists do not like British cooking.	

vocabulary	dt. Bedeutung	English sentence	syn/opp
crisps [BE]	*Chips*	Crisps are extremely unhealthy.	= chips [AE]
customer	*Kunde/Kundin*	The health food shop has a lot of new customers.	
dairy products	*Molkerei-erzeugnisse*	Some dairy products (such as cheese or creamy yogurt) contain a lot of fat.	
(to) damage	*schädigen*	Ecstasy pills damage brain cells.	≠ (to) cure, (to) heal
(to) declare declaration	*erklären, verkünden, bekanntmachen* *Erklärung*	The president declared the White House a smoke-free zone.	
diet (to) be/go on a diet	*Kost, Ernährung, Nahrung* *eine Diät machen*	Fruits and vegetables are part of a healthy diet. Michael wants to lose weight – he's going on a diet.	
(to) digest digestion	*verdauen* *Verdauung*	The foods you eat are broken down, or digested, inside your body into smaller and smaller pieces.	
dinner	*Abendessen, Abendbrot*	We normally have dinner at half past seven.	
disease	*Krankheit*	Doctors can cure many diseases today.	= illness
dish	*Gericht*	Many British families like to try new dishes.	= meal
	Schale, Schüssel, Platte	Carla served the meal on beautiful dishes.	= plate, bowl
drug	*Droge, Rauschgift*	Two of the biggest problems today are drugs and crime.	
	Medikament	Aspirin is one of the most widely used drugs.	= medicine

vocabulary	dt. Bedeutung	English sentence	syn/opp
eating disorder	Essstörung	Problems at home and at school can lead to eating disorders.	
(to) encourage	ermutigen, jmdm. Mut zusprechen	Adverts may encourage young people to start smoking.	≠ (to) discourage
energy	Energie	The body changes the calories in food into energy.	
exercise (to) get exercise	Bewegung sich bewegen	On the whole, the British get far too little exercise.	
fashionable	modisch, schick	A lot of parents think that their children drink because they find it fashionable.	
fat	Fett	Mayonnaise contains a lot of fat.	
fries [AE]	Pommes	Most people like ketchup with their fries.	= chips [BE]
habit	Gewohnheit	Think about your eating habits. Do you eat healthily?	
(to) harm	schädigen	Alcohol harms young people.	= (to) damage, (to) affect
harmful	schädlich	Smoking is extremely harmful.	= damaging
headache	Kopfschmerzen	Marc had a terrible headache. I gave him a tablet.	
health	Gesundheit	Too much fast food is bad for your health.	≠ illness, disease
healthy	gesund	Fast food is not very healthy.	
health care	Gesundheitsfürsorge	People live longer today because of better health care.	
hospital	Krankenhaus	The tourist who was hit by a London bus was taken to St Stephen's Hospital.	= clinic

vocabulary	dt. Bedeutung	English sentence	syn/opp
illegal	illegal, ungesetzlich, gesetzwidrig	Cocaine and heroin are illegal drugs.	≠ legal, lawful
(to) improve	verbessern, besser machen/werden	The government wants to improve people's health.	≠ (to) make worse
improvement	Verbesserung		
junk food	minderwertiges, ungesundes Essen	The government wants to stop TV adverts for junk food.	≠ healthy diet, healthy food
label	Etikett	Cigarette packages carry a warning label.	
lamb	Lamm(-fleisch)	In India a hamburger is made of lamb, because Hindus are not allowed to eat beef.	
lifestyle	Lebensstil, Lebensweise	A healthy lifestyle helps to avoid illness and suffering.	
lunch	Mittagessen	Daniel always cooks lunch and dinner for the family.	
meal	Mahlzeit	A large fast food meal has more than 1,300 calories.	
menu	Speisekarte	Our menu includes special dishes for people suffering from food allergies.	
non-smoking zone/area	Nichtraucherbereich	Most airports and public buildings are non-smoking areas.	
obesity	Fettleibigkeit	Childhood obesity is a serious health problem.	
obese	übergewichtig		= overweight
(to) offer	anbieten	Our school canteen tries to offer healthier food.	
offer	Angebot		
(to) order	bestellen	In some fast food restaurants today you can order fresh fruit and salads.	

vocabulary	dt. Bedeutung	English sentence	syn/opp
overweight	übergewichtig	Two thirds of British men are overweight.	= obese ≠ underweight
(to) provide	zur Verfügung stellen, liefern	Fresh fruit and vegetables provide the body with vitamins.	= (to) supply
(to) recommend recommenda- tion	empfehlen Empfehlung	It is recommended that you do some exercise every day.	= (to) advise
(to) reduce reduction	verringern Verringerung	The food industry should reduce the sugar content of their products.	≠ (to) increase
(to) restrict restriction	etwas beschrän- ken, einschränken Beschränkung	Drinking alcohol in public is restricted in many coun- tries.	= (to) limit
(to) save	sparen	Mick could save a lot of money if he didn't smoke.	≠ (to) spend, (to) waste
(to) shorten	verkürzen	Every cigarette you smoke shortens your life by seven to eleven minutes.	≠ (to) leng- then, (to) make longer, (to) ex- tend
soft drink	alkoholfreies Getränk	Soft drinks contain a lot of sugar but no alcohol.	
strict	streng	Stricter regulations about smoking in public were introduced in New York.	
supper	Abendessen	My sister and I always wash the dishes after supper.	
(to) taste taste tasty	schmecken Geschmack lecker	This tomato soup tastes delicious. I think I'd like some more, please.	
(to) treat treatment	behandeln Behandlung	Doctors diagnose and treat diseases.	

vocabulary	dt. Bedeutung	English sentence	syn/opp
vegan [i:]	*Veganer/-in*	People who do not eat any animal products are called vegans.	
vegetables	*Gemüse*	The doctor told Emily to eat more fruit and vegetables.	
vegetarian	*vegetarisch; Vegetarier/-in*	Most restaurants offer vegetarian dishes for people who do not eat meat.	
volunteer voluntary	*Freiwillige(r) freiwillig*	Many young people work in hospitals as volunteers because they want to help.	
waiter waitress	*Kellner Kellnerin*	There are no waiters or waitresses in fast food restaurants.	
(to) warn warning	*warnen Warnung*	The police warn people not to drink and drive.	
(to) weigh weight	*wiegen Gewicht*	How much do you weigh? Eating too much fat causes weight problems.	
(to) lose weight	*abnehmen*	If you eat less food than your body needs, you will lose weight.	= (to) go on a diet ≠ (to) put on weight, (to) gain weight
worry (to) worry	*Sorge, Kummer sich sorgen*	Too many worries can make people ill.	

Work

vocabulary	dt. Bedeutung	English sentence	syn/opp
achievement	Leistung, Erfolg, Errungenschaft	Finishing school with good marks is a major achievement.	
advice (to) advise	Rat raten	Before you choose a job, get some expert advice.	
application	Bewerbung	I handed in my application for a job with Barclays Bank yesterday.	
application form	Bewerbungs- formular	The secretary helped me to complete the application form.	
(to) apply for a job	sich um eine Stelle bewerben	After leaving school, Harry applied for a job with several firms.	
apprentice	Lehrling, Auszubildende(r)	If you want to learn your job properly, you should start as an apprentice.	
apprenticeship	Lehrzeit, Lehre, Ausbildung	During his apprenticeship Ed didn't earn a lot of money.	
assembly line	Fließband	On an assembly line, a car is put together one piece at a time.	= conveyor belt
bankrupt	bankrott, zahlungsunfähig	The firm went bankrupt because their product didn't sell any longer.	
blue-collar worker	Arbeiter/-in	People who work in factories are sometimes called blue-collar workers.	≠ white-collar worker, clerk
career	berufliche Lauf- bahn, Karriere	Do you think that a pupil has enough time to practise to have a career as a champion athlete?	

vocabulary	dt. Bedeutung	English sentence	syn/opp
careers adviser	Berufsberater/-in	Your local careers adviser helps you find out about training programmes in your area.	= careers officer
child labour	Kinderarbeit	Child labour is a big problem in poor countries, where young children work in factories.	
choice (to) choose	Wahl wählen	What would you like to do? The choice is yours.	
commerce	Handel, Verkehr	Commerce between Germany and China has grown.	= business, trade
commuter (to) commute	Pendler/-in pendeln	Commuters travel a long distance from home to work every day.	
company	Firma	The new video game will earn a lot of money for our company.	= business, firm
compatible	passend	Try to find a job which is compatible with your qualifications.	= suited ≠ incompatible, unsuited
conveyor belt	Montageband, Fließband	Tom Birch stands at a conveyor belt all day.	= assembly line
customer	Kunde/Kundin	The firm won new customers abroad.	= client
CV (curriculum vitae)	Lebenslauf	CV is short for the Latin "curriculum vitae".	= resume [AE]
(to) dismiss	entlassen, (jmdm.) kündigen	As the company had not made a profit, the manager had to dismiss 120 people.	= (to) discharge ≠ (to) employ, (to) hire
(to) earn one's living	seinen Lebensunterhalt verdienen	How do you earn your living?	

vocabulary	dt. Bedeutung	English sentence	syn/opp
(to) employ	*beschäftigen, anstellen*	The two largest firms in our town employ more than a thousand people each.	= (to) hire ≠ (to) dismiss, (to) discharge
employee	*Arbeitnehmer/-in, Angestellte(r)*	This company has more than 20,000 employees.	= worker
employer	*Arbeitgeber-/in*	The government is one of the largest employers in our country.	
employment	*Beschäftigung, Arbeit*	Lisa is looking for employment as a waitress.	≠ unemployment
equal opportunities [Pl.]	*Chancengleichheit*	Men and women should have equal opportunities at work.	≠ discrimination
factory	*Fabrik*	More people work in offices than in factories.	= works, shop, plant, mill
favourable	*positiv, günstig, sympathisch*	Large business firms use advertising to create a favourable image.	
(to) fire [colloquial]	*feuern, rausschmeißen*	The unsuccessful manager was fired by the directors.	= (to) sack [colloquial] ≠ (to) hire
(to) fill a position	*eine Stelle besetzen*	IBM is looking for a university graduate to fill the position of sales manager.	
full-time	*Vollzeit, ganztägig, Ganztags-*	Mary and Sean have just got married and they both work full-time.	≠ part-time
full-time job	*Vollzeit-, Ganztagsarbeit*	James gave up his full-time job to spend more time with his baby daughter.	≠ part-time job
gap year	*freies Jahr (meist zwischen dem Schulabschluss und dem Beginn des Studiums)*	In her gap year, Ashley travelled all around Australia.	

vocabulary	dt. Bedeutung	English sentence	syn/opp
income	Einkommen, Einkünfte	Many people who work in the City of London have a high income.	
industry	Industrie(-zweig), Gewerbe	The shipbuilding industry is in great trouble today.	
industrial	industriell		
job	Beruf, Beschäftigung, Stelle	Rita has found an exciting job as a tourist guide in York.	= employment, work, occupation
job centre	Arbeitsamt	The job centre offers summer jobs for young people.	= labor office [AE]
job experience	Berufserfahrung	The employer asked Milo about his job experience as a programmer.	
job interview	Vorstellungsgespräch	Before you go to a job interview, try to get as much information as possible about the firm in question.	
job market	Arbeitsmarkt	What effect will robots have on the job market?	= labour market, employment market
job sharing	Arbeitsplatzteilung, Stellenteilung	Job sharing is a way for two people to fill one post. Each person has a permanent part-time post.	
labour	Arbeit, Arbeitskräfte	Many firms have their production in Asia or Africa because labour is cheaper there.	
(to) live on	leben von	Danny, who works in a fast food restaurant, has very little money to live on.	
(to) maintain	aufrechterhalten, bewahren	The motor company works hard to maintain the quality of its cars.	
maintenance	Bewahrung		

vocabulary	dt. Bedeutung	English sentence	syn/opp
(to) manufacture manufacturer manufactured goods	herstellen, erzeugen Hersteller Fertigwaren	Chemists can manufacture substances that do not exist naturally. Britain sold manufactured goods to her colonies.	= (to) make, (to) produce = finished products
minimum wage	Mindestlohn	The minimum wage is often not enough to live on.	
model	Modell, Mannequin	Meg dreams of working as a fashion model.	
notice (to) hand in one's notice (to) give notice without notice	Kündigung selbst kündigen jmdm. kündigen fristlos	Dan did not like his job at the airport so he handed in his notice. To make production cheaper the company gave notice to 50 employees. As he had stolen some tools from the shop floor, Angus was dismissed without notice.	
offer (to) offer	Angebot anbieten	Liam accepted the new job offer.	
order (to) order	Bestellung, Auftrag bestellen	We thank you for your order of 25 laptops and tablet PCs.	
output	Ausstoß, Arbeitsleistung	The daily output of cars at the new plant in Leipzig has gone up to 950 units.	
overtime (to) work overtime	Überstunden Überstunden machen	Mr Growney is working overtime because his colleague is ill.	
part-time	Teilzeit-, Halbtags-	Natalie has a part-time job because she has to look after her baby son.	≠ full-time
pay(ment)	Bezahlung, Lohn	Vince works as a security guard but his pay is rather low.	= wages, salary

vocabulary	dt. Bedeutung	English sentence	syn/opp
perspective	*Perspektive, Blickwinkel*	It was a good job from a financial perspective.	
plant	*Anlage, Werk*	iPad screens are produced in a new plant in China.	= works, factory, mill
position	*Stellung*	Ian Morris took up his position as Assistant Manager in January.	= post, job
(to) produce	*herstellen, erzeugen*	Our company produces thousands of cars every year.	= (to) make, (to) manufacture
production	*Herstellung*		
productive	*produktiv, ertragreich, rentabel*		≠ unproductive
(to) promote	*befördern*	Sarah Murphy was promoted to Deputy Staff Manager.	
promotion	*Beförderung*	You have to work hard in order to get a promotion.	
prospect	*Aussicht, Chance*	School-leavers with good marks have better prospects of getting a job soon.	= chance, opportunity, possibility
(to) qualify	*sich qualifizieren*	Debbie Winter studied three languages so she could qualify as a translator.	
qualification	*Eignung; Vorbildung*	If you do not have good qualifications, it can be very hard to find a job.	
(to) quit	*(selbst) kündigen*	Jamie quit her job as a kitchen help after nine days.	= (to) resign
regular job	*feste Stelle*	Gregory has a regular job as a mechanic.	
(to) resign	*selbst kündigen*	The chairman will resign next month.	
resignation	*Kündigung*		

vocabulary	dt. Bedeutung	English sentence	syn/opp
(to) retire retirement	in Pension/Rente gehen, sich pensionieren lassen Rente, Pension	My grandfather doesn't work anymore – he retired last year.	≠ (to) start work
rise (to) get a rise	Lohnerhöhung eine Lohnerhöhung bekommen	Brian Kelly has just got a rise of £ 50 a month.	
(to) run a firm	eine Firma leiten	Jim Goodwin has run his firm for 23 years now.	
salary	Gehalt	Donna Birch's salary has gone up to £ 34,900 a year.	
shift	(Arbeits-)Schicht	All his life William Peel has been working the night shift.	
skill skilful	Fertigkeit, Qualifikation erfahren, geschickt	Our course is for people who wish to improve their skills and knowledge.	
skilled worker	Facharbeiter/-in	A skilled worker has greater chances of finding a good job.	≠ unskilled worker
staff	Belegschaft	The director was pleased with the good work of the staff.	= workforce
staff manager	Personalchef/-in	I'd like to talk to the staff manager about my complaint, please.	= personnel manager; human resources (HR) director
stressful	anstrengend, aufreibend, stressig	Working as a nurse can be very stressful.	≠ relaxing
strike (to) call a strike	Streik einen Streik ausrufen	If talks fail, the union will call a strike.	

vocabulary	dt. Bedeutung	English sentence	syn/opp
sweatshop	*Ausbeutungs-betrieb*	In most sweatshops, the working conditions are really bad.	
(to) sweat	*schwitzen*	In Pakistan, even young children have to work long hours, sweating in the terrible heat.	
tool	*Werkzeug, Gerät*	If you want to repair this old car, you'll need the right tools.	
trade	*Handel, Handels-verkehr* *Beruf (im Hand-werk)*	Trade between Europe and China has increased. James Dyar told his son to learn a proper trade.	= commerce, business = job
by trade	*von Beruf*	Oliver McDonald is a mechanic by trade.	
trade union	*Gewerkschaft*	In the 19th century the first trade union was formed in England.	= labor union [AE]
trainee	*Praktikant/-in, Azubi, Lehrling*	Claire works as a trainee reporter for "The Global News".	
training	*Ausbildung*	When Richard started in his new job, he was first given computer training.	
unemployed	*arbeitslos*	Unemployed school-leavers get help from the government.	= jobless, out of work
unemployment	*Arbeitslosigkeit*	Unemployment is a big problem in some countries.	
unskilled	*ungelernt, nicht ausgebildet*	Unskilled workers can lose their jobs quickly.	≠ skilled
vacancy vacant	*freie/offene Stelle* *frei*	Martin Beadle, who is a trained carpenter, has been looking for a vacancy in his area for months.	

vocabulary	dt. Bedeutung	English sentence	syn/opp
volunteer	*Freiwillige(r)*	Amy worked as a volunteer in an animal shelter in Canada.	
wage	*(Arbeits-)Lohn*	The government wants to raise the minimum wage.	= pay
weakness	*Schwäche*	Paul knows that maths is one of his weaknesses.	≠ strength
white-collar worker	*Büroangestellte(r)*	People who work in offices or banks are called white-collar workers.	= clerk ≠ blue-collar worker
work (to) be out of work	*Arbeit arbeitslos sein*	Being out of work for a long time makes people feel depressed.	
working conditions	*Arbeits- bedingungen*	The trade unions fight for better working conditions.	
(to) work shifts	*Schicht arbeiten*	In our printing plant, we work 24-hour shifts.	
workshop	*Workshop, Seminar*	Are you interested in a workshop on computer programming?	
	Werkstatt	The mechanic is in his workshop every day.	

Immigration and Minorities

vocabulary	dt. Bedeutung	English sentence	syn/opp
(to) abandon	*aufgeben, preis-geben, verlassen*	We must not abandon children from poor families.	= (to) leave alone
(to) abolish	*abschaffen*	Slavery was abolished in the US in 1865.	
abolitionist	*Gegner/-in der Sklaverei (auch der Todesstrafe)*	People who worked to end slavery were called abolitionists.	
(to) admit	*zulassen, zuge-ben, zugestehen*	In 1957, the first African American students were admitted to an all-white high school.	
admission	*Zulassung, Eintritt*		
adventure	*Abenteuer*	Many immigrants came to America looking for adventure or better living conditions.	
afraid	*verängstigt*	A lot of African Americans are afraid of becoming the victims of police violence.	
(to) be afraid	*befürchten*		
African American	*Afro-Amerikaner/-in*	On average, African Americans still earn less than white Americans.	
alien	*Fremde(r), Ausländer/-in; Außerirdischer*	Vicky was treated like an alien in her new neighbourhood.	= foreigner, stranger ≠ native
(to) allow	*erlauben*	Foreigners need a "green card" to be allowed to live and work in the USA permanently.	= (to) permit
allowance	*Erlaubnis*		
ancestor	*Vorfahr/-in*	Most Americans have ancestors who came from overseas.	≠ descendant

vocabulary	dt. Bedeutung	English sentence	syn/opp
annual	*jährlich, Jahres-*	The annual number of immigrants to the US is about 1 million.	= yearly
anxiety	*Angst, Besorgnis*	Anxiety about jobs is not unusual among young African Americans.	= worry, concern
anxious	*besorgt*	Jessica was anxious about getting a new job.	
appearance	*Erscheinung, Aussehen*	One shouldn't judge people by their appearance.	= looks
(to) appear	*erscheinen*		
area	*Gebiet, Bereich*	More Hispanics moved into the Miami area.	= district
(to) argue	*argumentieren; streiten*	Most scientists argue that cultural diversity enriches societies.	
argument	*Argument; Wortwechsel, Streit*	Many arguments against immigration are not justified.	
(to) arise	*sich ergeben, entstehen*	Problems arise when people do not trust each other.	= (to) develop, (to) start
(to) arrive arrival	*ankommen Ankunft*	The first Europeans arrived in the Americas in 1492.	≠ (to) leave, (to) depart
ashamed	*beschämt*	Manuel felt ashamed because his parents were very poor.	≠ proud
(to) ask for	*bitten um*	Poor people are often too ashamed to ask for help.	
attitude	*Haltung, Einstellung*	Attitudes towards immigration are changing.	= view, opinion
(to) attract attraction attractive	*anziehen Anziehungskraft anziehend*	Many states tried to attract settlers.	

vocabulary	dt. Bedeutung	English sentence	syn/opp
average on average	*durchschnittlich,* *Durchschnitts-* *im Durchschnitt*	The average immigration increased in the 19th century.	
baggage [AE]	*Gepäck*	The emigrants went on board carrying their baggage on their backs.	= luggage [BE]
because of	*wegen*	Fewer immigrants came to the US in the 1960s because of new, stricter laws.	= due to
(to) belong	*gehören,* *angehören*	A mixed marriage is a marriage in which partners belong to different races or religions.	
below	*unter, unten*	On average, more black than white people live below the poverty line.	≠ above
(to) blame	*die Schuld geben*	Some people blame foreigners for their own problems.	
border	*Grenze*	Illegal immigrants are caught at the US-Mexican border.	= frontier
burden	*Last*	Some right-wing politicians claim that immigrants are a financial burden on the country.	
by birth	*von Geburt*	Peter Meier became an American citizen but he was German by birth.	
cause	*Grund, Anlass*	Wars, terrorism and poverty are the main causes of people fleeing their home countries.	
(to) cause	*verursachen*		= (to) bring about

vocabulary	dt. Bedeutung	English sentence	syn/opp
century	*Jahrhundert*	The 19th century was a time of great industrial growth in the United States.	
citizen	*Staatsbürger/-in*	Until 1971 Commonwealth citizens could settle freely in the UK.	
civil right	*Bürgerrecht*	An important civil right is the right to vote.	
civil rights movement	*Bürgerrechts-bewegung (in den USA)*	Martin Luther King was the most important leader of the civil rights movement.	
clash	*Zusammenstoß*	There were clashes between police and protesters.	= riot, battle
community	*Gemeinde, Gemeinschaft*	New York City has the largest Jewish community outside Israel in the world.	
concerned	*besorgt, betroffen*	American workers are concerned about the competition of cheap labour.	= worried
(to) criticise criticism critic	*kritisieren Kritik Kritiker/-in*	Civil rights leaders criticised the new immigration law.	≠ (to) praise
(to) deny denial	*verweigern, leugnen Verweigerung, Leugnen*	We mustn't deny anybody the right to vote.	= (to) refuse ≠ (to) grant
descendant	*Nachfahre/ Nachfahrin*	Every year many descendants of immigrants visit Ellis Island.	≠ ancestor
desperate	*verzweifelt*	In the 19th century people in Ireland lived in desperate conditions.	

vocabulary	dt. Bedeutung	English sentence	syn/opp
(to) differ	*sich unter-scheiden*	Immigration laws differ from one country to another.	
difference	*Unterschied*		
different	*verschieden*		≠ same, equal
disadvantage	*Nachteil*	Black children had to face more disadvantages than white children.	≠ advantage
(to) be at a disadvantage	*benachteiligt sein*	In very conservative socie-ties, women are often at a disadvantage.	
disagreement	*Uneinigkeit*	The Puritans left England because of disagreements with the Church of Eng-land.	≠ agreement
(to) disagree	*nicht zustimmen*		
discrimination	*unterschiedliche Behandlung, Benachteiligung*	Discrimination between men and women at work is against the law.	≠ equality, equal oppor-tunities
(to) discriminate	*benachteiligen*		
Ellis Island	*Insel vor New York, von 1892 bis 1943 Kontrollstelle für Einwanderer*	In the 19th and 20th centu-ries 17 million immigrants arrived at Ellis Island.	
emigrant	*Auswanderer/ Auswanderin*	Emigrants are people who leave their home countries to live somewhere else.	≠ immigrant
(to) emigrate	*auswandern*	The "Mayflower" was full of people who wanted to emigrate to America.	≠ (to) immi-grate
emigration	*Auswanderung*		≠ immigration
equal	*gleich*	All men are created equal.	≠ unequal
equality	*Gleichheit*		≠ inequality
equal oppor-tunities [Pl.]	*Chancengleich-heit*	Many non-white people still do not enjoy equal opportu-nities at work.	≠ discrimi-nation
equal pay	*gleiche Bezahlung*		
ethnic	*ethnisch, Volks-*	There are a lot of different ethnic groups in the USA.	

vocabulary	dt. Bedeutung	English sentence	syn/opp
ethnic minority	ethnische Minderheit	The two largest ethnic minority groups in Britain are Asian and black people.	
explorer (to) explore exploration	Forscher/-in erforschen Erforschung	The explorer Christopher Columbus arrived at the New World in 1492.	
ferry	Fähre	A ferry transported the immigrants from Ellis Island to New York.	
flight (to) flee	Flucht fliehen	People went to America in the flight from poverty.	
foreign	ausländisch	Foreign workers need a visa or green card to take up work in the USA.	= from abroad, overseas
foreigner	Ausländer		= alien
fortune	Vermögen; Schicksal	Gold-digger Norman Felt made a fortune in Alaska.	
fortunate	glücklich, vom Schicksal begüns- tigt	I consider myself fortunate to be living in a peaceful country.	= lucky
founding fathers	Gründerväter	The founding fathers of the United States were men like Franklin, Jefferson and Washington.	
frontier	Grenze, Grenz- gebiet	The frontier in the West of the USA was considered to be the borderline between civilisation and wilderness.	= border
green card	Aufenthalts- erlaubnis	A green card allows you to stay in the US and work.	
(to) guard guard	bewachen Wächter/-in	The coasts and borders of the US are guarded day and night.	= (to) control

vocabulary	dt. Bedeutung	English sentence	syn/opp
hate (to) hate	*Hass* *hassen*	Love is the opposite of hate.	= hatred ≠ love
heritage (to) inherit hereditary	*Erbe* *erben* *Erb-*	Most Americans are very proud of their heritage.	
Hispanics	*Hispano-* *Amerikaner*	Hispanics (people from Spanish-speaking countries) are America's largest minority.	
homeland	*Heimatland,* *Vaterland*	Many Jamaicans left their homeland because they couldn't find work.	= mother country
homeless	*obdachlos*	Jack is one of many homeless people living in the streets of Los Angeles.	
hostility	*Feindschaft,* *Feindseligkeit*	Education can help to overcome prejudice and hostility between different ethnic groups.	≠ friendship
hostile	*feindlich*		≠ friendly
human rights	*Menschenrechte*	The basic human rights are the right to life and liberty.	
illegal	*ungesetzlich,* *rechtswidrig*	It is illegal to enter the US without documents.	= undocumented ≠ legal, lawful
immigrant	*Einwanderer/* *Einwanderin*	Many immigrants came to the US in search of freedom.	≠ emigrant
immigrant labour (to) immigrate	*zugewanderte* *Arbeitskräfte* *einwandern*	Some companies exploit cheap immigrant labour. After 1820, more people began to immigrate.	≠ (to) emigrate
immigration immigration law	*Einwanderung* *Einwanderungs-* *gesetz*	A new immigration law was passed by Congress.	≠ emigration = immigration bill/act

vocabulary	dt. Bedeutung	English sentence	syn/opp
(to) increase	*steigern, erhöhen, zunehmen*	In 1990 the US government announced a plan to increase immigration.	≠ (to) decrease, (to) reduce, (to) limit
increase	*Erhöhung, Zunahme*	The population increase in 1900 was due to millions of immigrants who entered the country at that time.	
increasing	*zunehmend, steigend*		
(to) intimidate	*einschüchtern, Angst einjagen*	Illegal workers can be intimidated easily.	= (to) scare, (to) frighten
jealous **jealousy**	*eifersüchtig* *Eifersucht*	One shouldn't be jealous of other people's successes.	
journey	*Reise*	From 1882 to 1902 more than two million immigrants made the journey from Bremen to New York.	
language	*Sprache*	Foreigners should learn the language of the country they emigrate to.	
(to) leave	*verlassen*	He had to leave the country within 72 hours.	= (to) get out of, (to) exit
liberty	*Freiheit*	The Statue of Liberty was presented by the French people to the Americans.	= freedom
(to) limit	*begrenzen*	A new law limits the number of newcomers.	= (to) restrict
low-paid job	*schlecht bezahlte Arbeit*	Many immigrants had to take low-paid jobs.	
majority	*Mehrheit*	The majority of the immigrants came to start a new life.	≠ minority
melting pot	*Schmelztiegel*	Americans liked to believe that their country was a melting pot of nations.	

vocabulary	dt. Bedeutung	English sentence	syn/opp
migration	*Migration, Wanderung*	The migration of black Americans to the cities in the North began after World War II.	
minority	*Minderheit*	The United Kingdom has a large black minority.	≠ majority
misery	*Elend, Not*	Racial conflicts brought misery to many families.	= unhappiness
mix (to) mix mixture mixed neigh- bourhood	*Mischung mischen Mischung, Gemisch gemischte Wohngegend*	The modern nation is a mix of cultures and races. Britain today is a curious mixture of past and present. We live in a mixed neigh- bourhood. Our neighbours are from India, Pakistan and Jamaica.	
multi-ethnic	*multiethnisch, Menschen ver- schiedener Her- kunft umfassend*	The US is a multi-ethnic society.	= (ethnically) diverse
native Native Americans	*einheimisch, (Ur-) Einwohner/-in Indianer, amerikanische Ureinwohner*	The Native Americans are the indigenous population of the US. "Native Americans" is the politically correct term for the indigenous population in the US.	= indigenous
neighbourhood	*Nachbarschaft*	In our neighbourhood, people from different countries live together.	
newcomer	*Neuankömmling*	Many newcomers did not find what they had expected.	= a person who has re- cently arrived
nightmare	*Alptraum*	For many immigrants life in the US began as a night- mare.	= an unplea- sant, terrible dream

vocabulary	dt. Bedeutung	English sentence	syn/opp
non-violent	*gewaltlos*	Martin Luther King always supported non-violent resistance.	≠ violent
(to) object to	*Einspruch erheben gegen*	The Pilgrims objected to some of the beliefs of the Church of England.	≠ (to) approve of, (to) agree to
(to) oppose	*sich wenden gegen, gegen etwas sein*	The northern states began to oppose slavery.	≠ (to) agree to, (to) accept
opposition	*Widerstand*	The new law met with a lot of opposition.	≠ approval
opposite	*Gegenteil gegenüber, ent- gegengesetzt*	Hate is the opposite of love. The immigration office can be found in the opposite building.	
oppressed **oppression**	*unterdrückt* *Unterdrückung*	We should support op- pressed people in their fight for equal rights.	= suppressed, persecuted
outlaw	*Geächtete(r), Vogelfreie(r)*	The outlaw Jesse James formed a gang.	= bandit, criminal
(to) overcome	*überwinden, bewältigen*	It is necessary to overcome racism and other forms of discrimination.	
(to) persecute **persecution**	*verfolgen* *Verfolgung*	People who felt persecuted left their homelands. Jamal's family had to flee from persecution.	
pilgrim	*Pilger/-in*	The Pilgrim Fathers sailed on board the Mayflower from Plymouth (England) to the New World.	
populated **(to) populate** **population**	*bevölkert* *bevölkern* *Bevölkerung*	Brixton is populated mainly by black people. In the 19th century, Lon- don's population grew from 1 to over 5 million.	= inhabited

vocabulary	dt. Bedeutung	English sentence	syn/opp
poverty	*Armut*	German farmers went to America to escape from poverty.	≠ riches, wealth
poor	*arm*	The gap between rich and poor people is widening.	≠ rich, wealthy
prejudice	*Vorurteil*	It is shocking how many people have prejudices against foreigners.	
(to) be prejudiced against	*Vorurteile haben gegenüber*	Too many people are still prejudiced against minorities.	
prospect	*Aussicht, Chance*	People should have the same educational or job prospects, regardless of their gender, race or sexual orientation.	= chance, hope
pursuit	*Streben, Trachten*	The US Declaration of Independence guarantees the right to the pursuit of happiness.	
questionnaire	*Fragebogen*	The immigrants had to fill in a questionnaire.	
race	*„Rasse"*	In English, the term "race" is often used to refer to a person's skin colour or origin. However, some people find this quite problematic.	
race relations	*Rassenbeziehungen, ethnische Beziehungen*	The problem of unemployment has made race relations worse in the last few years.	
racial	*„rassisch", „Rassen-"*	Malcolm X believed that racial justice for blacks could be achieved.	
racial problem	*Rassenproblem*	There are still serious racial problems in Britain today.	= racial conflict

vocabulary	dt. Bedeutung	English sentence	syn/opp
racial segregation	Rassentrennung	The Supreme Court decided that racial segregation in schools is against the constitution.	= separation, discrimination ≠ integration
racial tension	Rassenspannung	Racial tension increased after there had been attacks by white policemen on black protesters.	
racism	Rassismus	We need to fight all forms of racism.	
racist	Rassist/-in	Four black schoolgirls were killed by a white racist.	
refugee	Flüchtling	When people first come to a country they are often taken to a refugee camp.	
resistance (to) resist resistant	Widerstand sich widersetzen widerstandsfähig	Martin Luther King used Gandhi's method of non-violent resistance.	= opposition
respect respected respectable	Achtung, Respekt geachtet anständig	Martin Luther King won the respect of many white Americans.	
respect respectively	Hinsicht, Beziehung beziehungsweise	In this respect, M. L. King was different from Malcolm X, who was seen far more critically by most white people.	
restriction	Ein-, Beschränkung	Canada introduced restrictions on the number of immigrants.	= limitation
(to) restrict restrictive	beschränken einschränkend		= (to) limit
riot	(Straßen-)schlacht, Krawall	Riots broke out after Martin Luther King was shot.	= fight, clash
rival	Konkurrent/-in	Newcomers were often seen as rivals.	= competitor ≠ partner

vocabulary	dt. Bedeutung	English sentence	syn/opp
scared	verängstigt	A lot of refugees who have fled from war are scared of being sent back.	= frightened, afraid
(to) scare	erschrecken		= (to) frighten
search (to) search	Suche suchen	People have always come to America in search of a better life.	
segregation	Rassentrennung	Racial segregation is against the constitution.	= separation ≠ integration
(to) separate [eit]	trennen, (ab)teilen	Black children and white children were separated at school.	
separate [ət]	getrennt, abgesondert	Black and white children went to separate schools.	
(to) settle	sich niederlassen, besiedeln	The first English immigrants settled at Jamestown, Virginia, in 1607.	
settler	Siedler/-in	The Pilgrim Fathers were among the first white settlers in America.	
settlement	Siedlung, Niederlassung	The settlement was surrounded by a fence.	
shelter	Schutz, Schutzraum	Many poor people do not have enough food, clothing or shelter.	= house, roof, protection
slavery	Sklaverei	Thousands of Native Americans were killed in wars or forced into slavery.	≠ freedom, liberty
(to) slow down	verringern, verlangsamen	The Immigration Bill of 1971 slowed down the immigration of people from Commonwealth countries in Britain.	≠ (to) speed up
society social	Gesellschaft gesellschaftlich	There is still too much injustice in our modern society.	

vocabulary	dt. Bedeutung	English sentence	syn/opp
social worker	*Sozialarbeiter/-in*	Social workers try to help people in trouble.	
(to) spread	*ausbreiten, sich verbreiten*	The sad news of Martin Luther King's death spread rapidly.	
standard of living	*Lebensstandard*	Most Americans enjoy a high standard of living.	
(to) tackle	*fertig werden mit, (ein Problem) anpacken*	How will the president tackle the problem of the homeless and poor?	= (to) cope with
tension tense	*Spannung gespannt, spannend*	Social tensions between the rich and the poor are increasing.	
(to) threaten threat	*bedrohen Bedrohung*	Some immigrant workers were threatened by their white co-workers.	
tolerance tolerant (to) tolerate	*Duldsamkeit, Toleranz duldsam, tolerant dulden, tolerieren*	People should show more tolerance and respect towards foreigners.	
(to) treat treatment	*behandeln Behandlung*	Undocumented immigrants were treated badly.	
tribe	*(Volks-)Stamm*	The Havasupai tribe lived in the Grand Canyon region.	
trouble	*Problem, Schwierigkeit*	Many people have trouble finding affordable housing.	= problem
undocumented	*ohne gültige Papiere*	Undocumented workers will now get a new chance to stay in the USA.	= illegal ≠ legal
unwanted	*unerwünscht, störend*	Some immigrants felt unwanted.	
victim	*Opfer*	A new website helps victims of bullying.	

vocabulary	dt. Bedeutung	English sentence	syn/opp
violent	*gewalttätig; heftig*	Violent clashes between different gangs broke out last week.	≠ non-violent
violence	*Gewalt, Gewalttätigkeit*	Problems cannot be solved by violence.	≠ non-violence
welfare [AE]	*Sozialhilfe*	Many poor people in the US have to live on welfare.	= income support
work permit	*Arbeitserlaubnis*	If you want to work in the US, you need a work permit.	
(to) worry about	*sich Sorgen machen über*	Many Londoners worry about their safety on the Underground.	
xenophobia	*Ausländerfeindlichkeit*	We must try to overcome all kinds of xenophobia.	

Media

vocabulary	dt. Bedeutung	English sentence	syn/opp
account	*Benutzerkonto*	Even the Pope has an account on Facebook.	
actor, actress	*Schauspieler, Schauspielerin*	J. K. Rowling helped choose the actors for the first Harry Potter film.	
(to) advertise	*inserieren, werben*	People advertise in newspapers to sell houses or used cars.	
advertisement (ad or advert)	*Anzeige*	Advertisements take up a large part of newspapers and magazines.	
advertising campaign	*Werbekampagne, Werbefeldzug*	The company started a new advertising campaign to improve its image.	
advice column	*Ratgeberrubrik, -spalte (in Zeitschriften)*	A new advice column on our website offers answers to teenage problems.	
app(lication)	*Anwendung, App, Programm*	There are millions of apps for smartphones.	
article	*Artikel*	I read an interesting article about extreme sports in a magazine.	
audience	*Zuschauer, Publikum*	American football always has a large TV audience.	= viewers
BBC (British Broadcasting Corportation)	*TV-Sender in Großbritannien*	The BBC was founded in 1922.	
blog	*Blog, Internettagebuch*	Jeff is writing a blog while he is travelling China.	
box office	*Kino-, Theaterkasse*	The new film was a great box office success.	

vocabulary	dt. Bedeutung	English sentence	syn/opp
(to) broadcast	*senden, übertragen*	The cup final will be broadcast live on television.	= (to) transmit, (to) show
brochure	*Broschüre*	I sent for a brochure about Universal Studios.	= leaflet
cable TV	*Kabelfernsehen*	Cable TV uses wires to transmit signals.	
cast	*Besetzung (in einem Film)*	The cast of the latest Steven Spielberg film was interviewed by reporters.	
CCTV (closed circuit television)	*Video-überwachung*	The police use closed circuit television (CCTV) to keep watch on shops and city centres.	
censorship	*Zensur*	In a free state there is no censorship.	
channel	*(Fernseh-)Kanal, Programm*	Most TV channels are financed by advertising.	
(to) chat chat	*chatten; plaudern (Online-)Chat; Unterhaltung*	What is your favourite app for chatting with your friends?	
(to) choose choice	*auswählen Wahl*	In casting shows, viewers can choose their favourite singer by voting online.	
column	*Kolumne, (Zeitungs-)Spalte*	A column is a type of text in which the author (the columnist) expresses his/her personal opinion.	
commercial	*Werbesendung, -spot*	Commercials are often quite funny.	
(to) communicate communication	*etwas mitteilen Kommunikation*	A lot of young people use social media to communicate.	
contents (to) contain	*Inhalt enthalten*	The contents of the new film were long kept secret.	

vocabulary	dt. Bedeutung	English sentence	syn/opp
copy	*(Zeitungs-/ Buch-)Exemplar*	Today, newspapers sell fewer printed copies because a lot of people prefer the digital version.	
cover	*Bucheinband*	If a book has an interesting cover, people are more likely to buy it.	
(to) cover coverage	*berichten über Berichterstattung*	News coverage about the election campaign was really exciting.	
crew	*Besatzung, Mannschaft*	When the filming was finished, the director invited the whole crew out for a meal.	
cyberbullying	*Cybermobbing, Internetschikane*	If people are humiliated or threatened online, this is called cyberbullying.	
cybercrime	*Internet- kriminalität*	Some people use the anonymity of the internet to commit cybercrime.	
daily (news- paper)	*Tageszeitung*	Many British people read more than one daily (news- paper).	≠ weekly, monthly
device	*Gerät*	Apple presented a new device in 2010: the iPad.	= gadget
dish	*Satellitenschüssel*	A dish picks up radio and TV signals from a satellite.	= satellite dish
(to) distract	*ablenken*	Motorists mustn't use smartphones when driving because they distract them.	
(to) distribute distribution	*verteilen Verteilung, Vertrieb*	Books are distributed through bookstores, book clubs and the internet.	

vocabulary	dt. Bedeutung	English sentence	syn/opp
(to) edit	*herausgeben, bearbeiten*	The new collection of poems was edited by a famous writer.	
editor	*Redakteur/-in, Herausgeber/-in*	A journalist who is responsible for the final version of a text is called an editor.	
edition	*Ausgabe, Auflage*	The first edition of the Gutenberg Bible was printed in 1451/52.	
encyclopaedia	*(sehr großes) Lexikon, Enzyklopädie*	The online encyclopaedia Wikipedia gives information on many different subjects.	
entertainment (to) entertain	*Unterhaltung unterhalten*	Films, TV shows and video games are different forms of entertainment.	
extract (to) extract	*Auszug herausholen*	I read a short extract from the novel and it made me curious about the rest.	
feature	*Reportage, Beitrag*	Last night I watched an interesting feature about hurricanes on TV.	= report
	Funktion	Smartphones have more features than most people need.	
feedback	*Rückmeldung*	The TV company asked viewers for their feedback on the new show.	
file	*Datei*	You should regularly back up your files so that they can't get lost.	
folder	*Ordner*	You can create different folders on your computer to organise your files.	

vocabulary	dt. Bedeutung	English sentence	syn/opp
freedom of expression	*Meinungsfreiheit*	Freedom of expression is the right to say what you think.	
freedom of the press	*Pressefreiheit*	A democratic government protects the freedom of the press.	
front page	*Titelseite*	The news about the tropical storm appeared on the front page of all the papers.	
heading	*Überschrift*	Try to find a new heading for this paragraph.	= title
headline	*Schlagzeile*	The marriage of the pop star made the headlines in many newspapers.	
importance important	*Bedeutung, Wichtigkeit* *wichtig*	Film and pop stars know the great importance of the media.	
issue (to) issue	*(Zeitungs-)Ausgabe, Nummer* *herausgeben*	In our next issue we'll publish a full report on the latest computer games.	
landline	*Festnetz*	Fewer people use a landline phone today because most have smartphones.	
(to) launch	*starten, mit etwas beginnen*	The government is launching a new anti-smoking campaign.	= (to) start, (to) begin
letter to the editor	*Leserbrief*	Today, many people post comments online instead of writing a letter to the editor.	
live [ai]	*direkt, live*	The landing on the moon was shown live on TV.	≠ (pre)recorded

vocabulary	dt. Bedeutung	English sentence	syn/opp
mass media	*Massenmedien*	The mass media – television, radio, newspapers and the internet – play an important role in society.	
message	*Nachricht, Botschaft, Mitteilung*	On our website you can read other people's messages.	
mobile phone	*Handy*	How many mobile phones have you had up to now?	= cell phone [AE]
mysterious mystery	*rätselhaft, geheimnisvoll* *Geheimnis*	Hollywood made a film about the mysterious death of the Egyptian pharaoh Tutankhamen.	
national paper	*überregionale, d. h. im ganzen Land gelesene Zeitung*	National papers such as "The Guardian" or "The Times" are read everywhere in the UK.	≠ regional paper, local paper
network	*Netz, Netzwerk*	Our firm has a computer network which allows all users to share information.	
news	*Nachricht(en)*	Have you heard the news today?	
newsletter	*Newsletter, Rundbrief*	Most internet sellers publish a monthly newsletter.	
online advertising	*Werbung im Internet*	Companies like Google earn a lot of money through online advertising.	= digital advertising
online shopping	*Einkaufen über das Internet, Onlineshopping*	Many consumers use the advantages of online shopping.	= internet-based shopping
paragraph	*(Text-)Absatz*	Try to summarise each paragraph in one sentence.	
(to) persuade persuasion	*überzeugen, überreden* *Überredung*	Big companies advertise to persuade people to buy their products.	

vocabulary	dt. Bedeutung	English sentence	syn/opp
(to) print **print**	*drucken* *Druck*	Gutenberg invented the technique of printing in the 1450s.	
bold print	*Fettdruck*	The instructions were written in bold print.	≠ small print
out of print	*vergriffen (z. B. ein Buch)*	I can't get that book because it is out of print.	
programme	*Sendung*	The BBC produces special programmes for children and young adults.	= show
(to) promote **promotion**	*fördern, für etwas werben* *Werbung, Werbekampagne*	Lots of companies use the internet to promote sales of their products.	
(to) prosecute **prosecution**	*gerichtlich verfolgen* *Verfolgung*	PC users who download films from the internet without paying will be prosecuted.	
(to) publish **publication** **publisher**	*veröffentlichen, herausgeben* *Veröffentlichung* *Verlag, Verleger*	An American company published a computer game based on the popular Lord of the Rings film. In the 1990s it was difficult for J. K. Rowling to find a publisher for her first Harry Potter book.	
quality (news)paper	*seriöse Tageszeitung*	The "Daily Telegraph" is a quality (news)paper.	≠ tabloid
reception	*Empfang*	Digital signals have made our TV reception much better.	
regional	*regional*	Britain has a large number of regional papers.	≠ national, nationwide
rehearsal **(to) rehearse**	*Probe* *proben*	Rehearsals for our new school play will start next week.	

vocabulary	dt. Bedeutung	English sentence	syn/opp
remote control	*Fernbedienung*	The first TV remote control was sold in the 1950s.	
report (to) report	*Bericht* *berichten*	The World Health Organisation published a new report about the dangers of alcohol.	
review (to) review	*Rezension, Kritik* *kritisieren, überprüfen*	The band's latest album received positive reviews.	
sale (to) sell	*Verkauf* *verkaufen*	Sales of the new video game have gone up.	
screen	*Bildschirm*	My father bought a TV set with a bigger screen.	
series	*Serie*	"Star Trek" is one of the most popular TV series.	
slogan	*Werbespruch*	The company slogan always appeared under the company name.	
soap opera	*Familienserie, Seifenoper*	The British TV soap opera "Coronation Street" was first shown in 1960.	
social media	*soziale Medien*	Facebook, Instagram and Snapchat are popular social media.	
(to) sponsor sponsor	*sponsern, finanziell unterstützen* *Sponsor/-in, Förderer/Förderin*	Some big companies sponsor sports events. It is often difficult for athletes to find sponsors.	= (to) finance
(to) switch off	*ausschalten*	If you find the show too boring, switch off the TV.	= (to) turn off ≠ (to) switch on
tabloid	*Boulevardzeitung, Klatschzeitung*	Tabloids like "The Sun" are known for their sensationalist style of journalism.	≠ quality paper

vocabulary	dt. Bedeutung	English sentence	syn/opp
television set / TV set	Fernsehapparat	Our neighbours are the only people I know who haven't got a television set.	
text (message)	SMS, Kurznachricht	Jordan doesn't reply to any of my texts – maybe he's forgotten his smartphone.	
(to) text	eine SMS / Kurznachricht schreiben	Could you text me when you get home?	
ticket	Karte	I'm trying to get a ticket for the football match next Sunday.	
ticket sale	Kartenverkauf	Ticket sales for the concert haven't started yet.	
(to) tune in	(ein Programm) einstellen, zuhören	We hope you'll tune in again next week when we look at the latest films.	
(to) turn down	(Lautstärke) leiser stellen	"Please turn your music down, Stewart."	
(to) turn off	(Radio, Fernseher) ausschalten	I was fed up with the silly programme, so I turned it off.	= (to) switch off
(to) turn on	(Radio, Fernseher) an-, einschalten	With a remote control you can turn on your TV set from where you are sitting.	= (to) switch on
tweet	Tweet	Tweets mustn't be longer than 140 characters.	
(to) tweet	twittern, einen Tweet schreiben	People often tweet about what they are doing at the moment.	
(to) unsubscribe	sich abmelden, abbestellen	You can unsubscribe from our newsletter at any time.	= (to) subscribe
user	Nutzer/-in, Anwender/-in	Facebook and Twitter have hundreds of millions of users.	

vocabulary	dt. Bedeutung	English sentence	syn/opp
username	*Benutzername*	Jenny's username is Jen2001.	
variety various	*Vielfalt* *vielfältig, ver- schieden*	Today we can choose from a variety of TV channels.	
viewer	*(Fernseh-) Zuschauer/-in*	Streaming services attract more and more viewers.	
volume	*Lautstärke*	A little switch allows you to control the volume of the player.	
volume	*Band (Buch)*	The Encyclopaedia Britannica has 35 volumes.	
(to) watch TV	*fernsehen*	How many hours a day do you watch TV?	
wireless internet	*WLAN, draht- loses Internet*	Most hotels offer wireless internet.	= Wi-Fi

Technology

vocabulary	dt. Bedeutung	English sentence	syn/opp
access	Zugang	More and more people around the world have access to the internet.	
(to) advance	voranschreiten	In computer games you advance from one level to the next.	= (to) progress
advance	Fortschritt		= progress
answering machine	Anrufbeant-worter	You can leave a message on an answering machine.	
artificial	künstlich	In 1957, the Soviets put the first artificial satellite into orbit.	≠ natural
atomic energy	Atomenergie	Is atomic energy the answer to our energy problems?	= nuclear energy
(to) be in favour of	befürworten, dafür sein	Are you in favour of the use of nuclear power?	≠ (to) be against
button	Knopf	"You push this button here to start the programme."	= key
at the push of a button	auf Knopfdruck	You can order things on-line at the push of a button.	
(to) cancel (an action)	(eine Aktion) abbrechen	If you want to cancel the action, press the escape key.	
(to) cause damage	Schaden verur-sachen	Computer viruses cause millions of dollars of da-mage every year.	
cell phone [AE]	Handy, Mobil-telefon	Can you call me on my cell phone, please?	= mobile phone [BE]
circle	Kreis	Strange circles appeared in cornfields over night.	

vocabulary	dt. Bedeutung	English sentence	syn/opp
(to) circle	umkreisen	The spaceship circled the moon.	
(to) click (on) a button	auf eine Schaltfläche klicken	Click this button to end the programme.	
clone	Klon, Nachbau	Scottish scientists produced clones – artificial twins – of animals.	
cloning	Klonen, Schaffung von erbgleichen Wesen	Cloning raises a lot of ethical questions.	
commander (to) command	Befehlshaber/-in befehlen, gebieten	James T. Kirk was made commander of the Starship Enterprise.	
complicated	kompliziert	My grandma finds computers too complicated.	= difficult, complex
computer application	Computeranwendung, Informatik	Paul did a computer application course at his school.	
computer scientist	Informatiker/-in	Computer scientists are working on the "thinking computer".	
(to) connect	verbinden	All of the PCs at our firm are connected to a central computer.	
connection	Verbindung	If you have a fast internet connection, you can download pictures quickly.	
contact	Verbindung, Kontakt	Mission Control in Houston lost contact with the Space Shuttle Columbia.	
(to) contact	kontaktieren, Verbindung aufnehmen	Please contact us if you need help.	
crash helmet	Sturzhelm	All motorcyclists must wear crash helmets.	

vocabulary	dt. Bedeutung	English sentence	syn/opp
(to) create **creation** **creature**	*(er-)schaffen* *Erschaffung* *Geschöpf*	The World Wide Web was created in the early 1990s.	
crew	*Mannschaft,* *Besatzung*	All seven crew members of the space shuttle were killed in the accident.	= team
cure **(to) cure**	*Heilung* *heilen*	Will there ever be a cure for cancer?	= remedy, medication
current	*aktuell*	The current prices for flat rates are still too high.	= present
data	*Daten, Angaben*	Be careful when somebody asks you for your personal data on the internet.	
data processing	*Daten-* *verarbeitung*	Data processing is carried out by computers.	
(to) delete	*löschen*	Benjamin deleted the document by mistake.	
(to) design **design**	*entwerfen,* *gestalten* *Entwurf,* *Gestaltung*	Helen learnt to design a webpage. I like the design of her new website.	
discovery **(to) discover**	*Entdeckung* *entdecken*	What is the most important scientific discovery or invention in your opinion?	
drive (in a computer)	*Laufwerk*	Does your laptop have a CD-ROM drive?	
(to) drive a car	*Auto fahren*	You have to pay to drive a car into central London.	
driving licence	*Führerschein*	My father has had his driving licence for more than thirty years.	
driving school	*Fahrschule*	Liz had a couple of lessons with the driving school before she took her test.	

vocabulary	dt. Bedeutung	English sentence	syn/opp
driving test	*Fahrprüfung*	In Britain you can take your driving test at 17.	
engine	*Motor*	Diesel engines are used for large vehicles.	= motor
engineer	*Ingenieur/-in, Konstrukteur/-in*	In 1876 the German engineer Nicolaus August Otto built a new type of engine.	
(to) engineer	*konstruieren, bauen*		
engineering	*Ingenieurwesen, Maschinenbau*	Lily studies engineering.	
(to) enter	*eingeben*	Please enter your user name and password here.	
entrance	*Eintritt, Zugang*		
entry	*Zutritt, Zugang*		
evolution	*Evolution, Entwicklung*	Charles Darwin developed the theory of evolution.	
(to) evolve	*sich entwickeln*	Science and technology evolve due to innovative ideas.	
(to) execute (a command)	*(einen Befehl) ausführen*	On a computer you execute a command with the enter key.	
execution	*Ausführung*		
expert	*Fachmann/ Fachfrau*	Some of my classmates are real computer experts.	= specialist
(to) explore	*erforschen*	People have always dreamed of exploring outer space.	
exploration	*Erforschung*		
(to) extend	*ausweiten*	Facebook wants to extend its business in China.	
(file) extension	*Dateiendung*	The extension of MS Word is *.doc or *.docx.	
extensive	*ausgedehnt, ausführlich*	Some apps make extensive use of private data.	
(to) fail a driving test	*bei einer Führerscheinprüfung durchfallen*	Poor old George failed his driving test twice.	≠ (to) pass a driving test

vocabulary	dt. Bedeutung	English sentence	syn/opp
folder	Verzeichnis, Ordner	I cannot remember in which folder I saved my essay.	= directory
(to) function	funktionieren	My new laptop computer functions perfectly.	= (to) work
gene	Gen	Gregor Mendel was one of the first people who studied genes.	
genetic engineering	Gentechnik	We hope that genetic engineering will help to cure illnesses.	
genetically modified food (GM food)	gentechnisch veränderte Nahrungsmittel	Many people think that genetically modified (GM) food is not good for us.	
global	global, weltweit	Global positioning systems (GPS) tell travellers where they are.	= worldwide
gravity	Schwerkraft	There is no gravity in outer space.	
(to) guide guidance	führen, leiten Leitung, Führung	A new technique was invented to guide and control a rocket.	
habitat	Lebensraum	Animals, plants and other organisms survive best in their natural habitat.	= environment, surroundings
hard disk	Festplatte	My music files take up a lot of space on my hard disk.	= hard drive
(to) infect infection	infizieren, anstecken Ansteckung	A computer virus infected computers around the world.	
(to) inherit	erben	Some people inherit illnesses from their parents.	
inheritance	Erbe	Gregor Mendel discovered the laws of inheritance.	

vocabulary	dt. Bedeutung	English sentence	syn/opp
inherited disease	*Erbkrankheit*	Haemophilia ("Bluter-krankheit") is an inherited disease.	
(on the) internet	*(im) Internet*	It is easy to find information on the internet.	= (on the) web
(to) install	*aufstellen, installieren*	ENIAC, a computer installed at the University of Pennsylvania in 1946, weighed about 30 tons.	= (to) set up ≠ (to) remove
(to) introduce introduction	*einführen Einführung, Einleitung*	Many firms introduce robots in order to produce more cheaply.	
(to) invent invention inventor	*erfinden Erfindung Erfinder*	The telephone was invented in 1876 by Alexander Graham Bell.	
isolated (to) isolate isolation	*einsam isolieren Isolation*	Do computer users become more isolated?	= lonely, lonesome
(to) keep in touch	*in Verbindung bleiben*	It is easy to keep in touch by sending messages.	≠ (to) lose touch/contact
key keyboard	*Taste Tastatur*	Press any key to continue. You can use the keyboard to type words and enter data into your computer.	= button
lane	*Spur*	In many cities there are special lanes for buses.	
(to) launch launch	*(eine Rakete usw.) starten Start*	In 1957 the Russians launched a satellite called Sputnik.	
level	*Niveau, Ebene*	Computer games are often divided into several levels.	
(to) limit limit limitation	*begrenzen Grenze Begrenzung*	Several space missions brought only limited success.	

vocabulary	dt. Bedeutung	English sentence	syn/opp
(to) manage	*(etwas) fertig-bringen*	Engineers managed to develop self-driving cars.	
means	*Mittel*		
means of communication	*Kommunikationsmittel*	Young people like using the latest means of communication.	
means of transport	*Verkehrsmittel*		
message	*Nachricht, Botschaft*	"Please leave your message after the tone."	
mobile (phone)	*Handy, Mobiltelefon*	Text messages can be sent by computer or mobile phone.	= cell phone [AE]
(to) modify	*ändern*	A computer virus can modify programmes.	= (to) change
operating system	*Betriebssystem*	"Windows" is the most widely used operating system for computers.	
(to) operate	*funktionieren*		
orbit	*Kreisbahn, Umlaufbahn*	The Russians put the first satellite into orbit around the Earth.	
(to) orbit	*umkreisen*		= (to) circle
(to) overtake	*überholen*	Jamie tried to overtake the lorry.	
(to) pass a driving test	*die Führerscheinprüfung bestehen*	Julie passed her driving test after 23 driving lessons.	≠ (to) fail a driving test
(to) paste	*einfügen*	You shouldn't copy-and-paste texts from the internet.	
	kleben, kleistern	We still need to paste the wall for the new wallpaper.	
(to) press a button	*eine Taste drücken*	Press this button to continue.	
printer	*Drucker*	In our firm we have five printers.	

vocabulary	dt. Bedeutung	English sentence	syn/opp
(to) process	*verarbeiten*	The computer processes a lot of information in seconds.	
(to) protect **protection**	*schützen* *Schutz*	In space astronauts must wear special clothing to protect themselves.	
race	*Wettlauf, Rennen*	In the 1950s the Americans and the Russians started the race into space.	
(to) receive **receiver** **reception**	*empfangen* *Empfänger* *Empfang*	With smartphones you can send and receive pictures. The reception is quite bad here.	
(to) recognise **recognition**	*erkennen* *(An-)Erkennung*	Some computers can recognise speech.	
(to) record	*aufzeichnen, aufnehmen*	My dad sometimes records television programmes if they start after 11 at night.	
(to) rely on	*sich verlassen auf*	Today, all industries rely on computers.	
(to) research **research** **researcher**	*forschen* *Forschung* *Forscher/-in*	Scientists research ways of finding cures for illnesses.	
(to) ride a bike	*Rad fahren*	In university towns many students ride bikes.	= (to) cycle
ring tone	*Klingelton*	Some ring tones sound really awful.	
rocket	*Rakete*	The Saturn V rocket, which was used in the Apollo programme, was more than 110 metres tall.	
satellite	*Satellit*	Sputnik 1 was the first satellite in space.	

vocabulary	dt. Bedeutung	English sentence	syn/opp
(to) save	*(eine Datei) sichern, speichern*	Save all your English documents in the same folder.	= (to) store
safe	*sicher*	Try to keep your personal data safe.	≠ unsafe, dangerous
safety	*Sicherheit*	The control centre was worried about the safety of the astronauts.	
scientific **science**	*wissenschaftlich* *Naturwissenschaft*	The astronauts carried out scientific experiments.	
scientist	*Naturwissenschaftler/-in*	Robert Koch was a famous German scientist.	
sea level	*Meeresspiegel*	Death Valley in California is 86 metres below sea level.	
search engine **(to) search**	*Suchmaschine* *suchen*	Google is the most well-known internet search engine.	
seat belt	*Sicherheitsgurt*	All drivers and passengers must wear seat belts.	
(to) solve **solution**	*lösen, auflösen* *Lösung*	We use computers to solve scientific and engineering problems.	
space	*Weltraum, Raum*	Would you like to fly into space?	= outer space
space exploration	*Erforschung des Weltraums*	The age of space exploration began in 1957 with the Russian satellite Sputnik 1.	
space suit	*Raumanzug*	The astronauts had to wear space suits when they left their spaceship.	
space travel	*Raumfahrt*	Space travel began in the 1960s.	

vocabulary	dt. Bedeutung	English sentence	syn/opp
spaceship	*Raumschiff*	After landing their spaceship on the moon, the astronauts started their experiments.	
speed limit	*Geschwindigkeitsbegrenzung*	The speed limit in towns is 30 miles per hour.	
(to) store storage	*speichern Speicherung*	You can store more data on a DVD than on a CD.	= (to) save
surface	*Oberfläche*	The first man who walked on the surface of the moon was the American astronaut Neil Armstrong.	
technical technique technology	*technisch, fachlich, Fach- Technik Technologie*	These technical problems can only be solved by experts. In England, 14-year-olds have to take a test in information and communications technology.	
(to) text text (message)	*eine Textnachricht schreiben Textnachricht, SMS*	A lot of young people prefer texting to phoning. Writing text messages is often cheaper than calling.	
(to) trace	*aufspüren, ausfindig machen, finden*	You can trace friends and relatives on the web.	= (to) find
traffic	*Verkehr*	Big cities like London have a lot of traffic problems.	
traffic jam	*Verkehrsstau*	There was a traffic jam on the road to the city centre.	= congestion
traffic sign	*Verkehrszeichen*	The Romans put up the first traffic signs.	
(to) transmit	*übertragen*	A telephone transmits sounds via electric wires.	

vocabulary	dt. Bedeutung	English sentence	syn/opp
treatment **(to) treat**	*Behandlung* *behandeln*	Mrs Walton broke her leg and was taken to hospital for treatment.	
(to) turn off	*ausschalten*	It is very hard for some children to turn off their computer.	= (to) switch off ≠ (to) switch on, (to) turn on
vehicle	*Fahrzeug*	No vehicles are allowed into the city centre between 8 a.m. and 6 p.m.	
virtual	*virtuell*	An English website offers a virtual tour of Stonehenge.	
virus	*Virus*	Try to protect your computer from viruses.	= worm
wireless	*drahtlos*	Most laptops can use a wireless connection to the internet.	
workshop	*Werkstatt*	We have to send the broken machine to the workshop.	

Environment

vocabulary	dt. Bedeutung	English sentence	syn/opp
acid rain	saurer Regen	Acid rain damages our forests, buildings and rivers.	
(to) affect	betreffen, sich auswirken auf	Climate change will affect us all.	
alternative	Alternative, andere Möglichkeit	Wind energy is an alternative to atomic (nuclear) energy.	
appliance	Gerät	Household appliances use a lot of electricity.	
atmosphere	Atmosphäre	The atmosphere protects the Earth like a warming blanket.	
average	durchschnittlich, Durchschnitts-	The average temperature on Earth has increased.	
aware (to) be aware	bewusst (sich) bewusst sein	People have become aware how important it is to protect the environment.	≠ unaware
balance	Gleichgewicht	The balance of nature has been disturbed.	
biofuel	Biokraftstoff	Biofuels made from food crops are a matter of controversy.	= renewable fuel, biomass fuel
bottle bank	Glascontainer	Don't throw that bottle away. Take it to the bottle bank.	
carbon dioxide	Kohlendioxid	The greenhouse effect is caused when too much carbon dioxide is released into the air.	

vocabulary	dt. Bedeutung	English sentence	syn/opp
catastrophe	*Katastrophe*	The Florida hurricane was a catastrophe that destroyed many houses.	= disaster
climate climate change	*Klima* *Klimawandel*	Poorer, developing countries will suffer more from climate change than wealthy ones.	
(to) consume consumer consumption	*verbrauchen* *Verbraucher/-in* *Verbrauch*	We should try to consume less.	
(to) contaminate contamination	*verseuchen* *Verunreinigung,* *Verseuchung*	Many rivers and lakes were contaminated with chemicals.	= (to) pollute
creature (to) create	*Lebewesen* *(er-)schaffen*	People believe that a strange creature lives in the lake of Loch Ness.	
(to) depend on dependency, dependence dependent	*abhängen/ab-* *hängig sein von* *Abhängigkeit* *abhängig*	The industrialised countries depend on oil. A lot of tourist regions are dependent on an intact natural environment.	 ≠ independence ≠ independent
(to) destroy destruction destructive	*zerstören* *Zerstörung* *zerstörerisch*	Since the 1940s, about half the world's rainforests have been destroyed. The international community should work together to stop the destruction of the rainforests.	
detergent	*Reinigungsmittel*	Household detergents pollute our rivers.	

vocabulary	dt. Bedeutung	English sentence	syn/opp
developed countries	*Industriestaaten, Industrieländer*	The developed countries are producing too much waste.	= industrialised countries ≠ developing countries, Third World countries
(to) die out	*aussterben*	More rare animals are about to die out.	= (to) become extinct
(to) disappear disappearance	*verschwinden Verschwinden*	Dinosaurs have long disappeared from the Earth.	
disaster	*Unglück, Katastrophe*	The recent oil tanker accident was a disaster for the coastal towns.	= catastrophe
disposable bottle	*Einwegflasche*	Disposable bottles needn't be returned to the shop.	≠ returnable bottle
disposal	*Beseitigung, Entsorgung*	There are special containers for the disposal of nuclear waste.	
drought	*Dürre*	A drought is a long period of dry weather without any rain.	≠ flood
(to) dry up	*austrocknen, vertrocknen*	Because of the long drought many rivers have dried up.	
dump	*Müllhalde*	We should not use the oceans as cheap dumps.	= rubbish tip
(to) dump	*abladen, ablagern*	Old car tyres have been dumped into the river.	
dumping ground	*Müllhalde, -kippe*	Some nations use the oceans as a dumping ground for chemical waste.	
earthquake	*Erdbeben*	In 1906 an earthquake in San Francisco killed hundreds of people.	

vocabulary	dt. Bedeutung	English sentence	syn/opp
effect (to) effect effective	*Wirkung, Aus-wirkung* *bewirken* *wirkungsvoll*	What will be the effects of changing temperatures on plants and animals?	= conse-quence
emission	*Ausstoß*	All countries have to work together to reduce the emission of greenhouse gases.	
energy conservation	*Energieein-sparung*	Energy conservation is one of the most important tasks for a greener future.	
energy consumption	*Energieverbrauch*	The developed countries should reduce their energy consumption.	
energy efficiency	*Energieeffizienz*	We must improve the energy efficiency of our houses.	
energy source	*Energiequelle*	Wind, water power and solar energy are alternative energy sources.	
energy transition	*Energiewende*	The aim of energy transi-tion is to replace nuclear power and fossil fuels with alternative sources of energy.	
environment	*Umwelt*	Keep our environment clean.	= sur-roundings
environmental studies	*Umweltforschung*	Environmental studies show us how we can save our planet.	
environmen-talist	*Umwelt-schützer/-in*	Environmentalists worry about the fast disappea-rance of the rainforest.	= conser-vationist
environmentally aware	*umweltbewusst*	The number of young peo-ple who are environmen-tally aware is increasing.	

vocabulary	dt. Bedeutung	English sentence	syn/opp
environmentally friendly	umweltfreundlich	When shopping I make sure that the product I buy is environmentally friendly.	≠ polluting
evolution (to) evolve	Entwicklung, Evolution sich entwickeln	Charles Darwin developed the theory of "evolution by natural selection".	
exhaust exhaust fumes	Auspuff (Auto-)Abgase	The exhaust on my car needs repairing. The exhaust fumes from millions of cars pollute the air.	
(to) forbid	verbieten	It is forbidden to throw rubbish into a river.	≠ (to) permit, (to) allow
fossil fuel	fossiler Brennstoff	Coal, petroleum and natural gas are examples of fossil fuels.	
global warming	Erderwärmung	Most people today know about the dangers of global warming.	
greenhouse effect	Treibhauseffekt	The warming of the Earth's surface is also called the "greenhouse effect".	
greenhouse gases	Treibhausgase	Millions of cars produce greenhouse gases.	
hygiene	Hygiene	Hygiene standards in Third World countries are low.	
industrial waste	Industrieabfall	Until recently, some countries threw their industrial waste into the sea.	
junk	Müll, Abfall	Ed's room is filled with junk.	= trash, litter, refuse, waste
(to) load load	belasten Last	We have loaded our air with dangerous chemicals.	= burden
marine life	Meeresfauna, Meeresflora	Plastic waste in the ocean is a danger to marine life.	

vocabulary	dt. Bedeutung	English sentence	syn/opp
natural gas	*Erdgas*	Natural gas is transported with the help of pipelines.	
nuclear power plant	*Atomkraftwerk*	Germany decided to shut down all of its nuclear power plants.	= nuclear/atomic power station
nuclear waste	*Atommüll*	We need a safe place for nuclear waste.	
oil slick	*Ölteppich*	A large oil slick appeared after the tanker had hit a rock.	
overpopulation	*Überbevölkerung*	Overpopulation means that too many people are living in one place.	
ozone layer	*Ozonschicht*	The ozone layer is getting thinner over the Antarctic.	
(to) persuade	*überzeugen*	People should be persuaded to use paper bags instead of plastic ones.	
pesticide	*Schädlingsbekämpfungsmittel, Pflanzenschutzmittel*	Farmers use pesticides to kill insects and weeds.	
petrol [BE]	*Benzin*	Big cars use too much petrol.	= gas [AE]
petroleum	*Rohöl*	OPEC is short for "Organisation of Petroleum Exporting Countries".	
poisonous poison	*giftig* *Gift, Schadstoff*	Fish in the sea were killed by petrol and poisonous chemicals.	= toxic
polar ice caps	*Polkappen*	Two per cent of the Earth's water is locked up as ice in glaciers ("Gletscher") and the polar ice caps.	

vocabulary	dt. Bedeutung	English sentence	syn/opp
(to) pollute	verschmutzen	The burning of coal and oil pollutes the air.	= (to) conta-minate ≠ (to) clean
polluting	umweltschädlich	Why don't we use the energy from the sun? It is less polluting.	≠ environ-mentally friendly
pollution	Verschmutzung	In the 1950s and 1960s, nobody thought about pollution.	
power station	Kraftwerk	There was a serious accident at the Fukushima power station in Japan.	= power plant
(to) protect protection	schützen Schutz	A group of US and Japanese scientists wants to protect apes and rhinos.	= (to) guard, (to) safeguard
rainforest	Regenwald	Tropical rainforests cover 7 % of the Earth's surface.	
raw material	Rohstoff	We mustn't waste our raw materials.	= resources
(to) recycle recycling	recyceln, wieder aufbereiten Wiederverwertung	Specialist firms recycle bottles, plastic and paper. Recycling helps to save raw materials.	
(to) reduce reduction	verringern Verringerung	We must try to reduce the amount of waste.	
(to) release	freisetzen, freilassen	When coal and petroleum are burned, they release dangerous gases into the air.	= (to) set free
renewable	erneuerbar	Wind power is a renewable source of energy.	
(to) repair	reparieren	People should try to repair electronic devices rather than throw them away.	

vocabulary	dt. Bedeutung	English sentence	syn/opp
resources	*Bodenschätze, Ressourcen*	Coal, oil and wood are natural resources.	= raw materials
returnable bottle	*Mehrwegflasche*	Returnable bottles can be used again.	≠ disposable bottle
reusable	*wiederverwertbar*	Reusable packaging could help solve our waste problem.	
(to) reuse	*wiederverwenden*	Don't throw this plastic bag away – reuse it!	
rubbish [BE]	*Müll, Abfall*	Dealing with rubbish is an enormous problem today.	= litter, refuse; garbage [AE]
(to) save	*sparen; retten*	Think about how you could save electricity.	
scientist	*Wissenschaftler/-in*	Scientists study the effects of climate change.	
skin cancer	*Hautkrebs*	If you often stay in the sun for too long, you can develop skin cancer.	
solar energy	*Sonnenenergie*	In the future, people will use more solar energy.	
solar system	*Sonnensystem*	The Earth is different from all the other planets in our solar system.	
source source of energy	*Quelle Energiequelle*	Nuclear power is a clean but dangerous source of energy.	
species	*Art, Spezies*	Thousands of species could die out because of global warming.	
surface	*Oberfläche*	It is quite possible that the surface of the Earth will warm up by several degrees over the next century.	

vocabulary	dt. Bedeutung	English sentence	syn/opp
survival (to) survive	*Überleben* *überleben*	Animals in mountain areas have a better chance of survival.	
threat	*Bedrohung*	Poisonous chemicals are a threat to our oceans.	= menace, hazard, risk
(to) threaten	*bedrohen*	The coastal cities were threatened by flooding.	= (to) endanger
toxic waste	*Giftmüll*	Where shall we put our toxic waste?	= poisonous rubbish
village	*Dorf*	The village uses the water power from the river to produce electricity.	
waste	*Abfall*	Some large firms have not done much about waste yet.	= junk, litter, rubbish, refuse
(to) waste	*vergeuden*	Don't waste energy.	
waste paper	*Altpapier*	Waste paper is a valuable raw material.	
waste separation	*Mülltrennung*	In Germany, waste separation is quite common.	
waste water	*Abwasser*	Waste water must not flow into our rivers.	= sewage
wind energy	*Windenergie*	We will need more wind energy when oil runs out.	
wind farm	*Windpark*	Some people say that wind farms spoil the landscape.	= wind park

Politics and Institutions

vocabulary	dt. Bedeutung	English sentence	syn/opp
agreement (to) agree	Vereinbarung, Übereinkunft übereinstimmen, zustimmen	After long discussions we came to an agreement.	≠ disagree-ment
(to) argue	sich streiten, zanken	Daniel and Josh are always arguing about their political views.	= (to) quarrel, (to) fight
(to) arrest	festnehmen, verhaften	A 25-year-old man was arrested because he had shot John Lennon.	≠ (to) set free, (to) release
armed forces	Streitkräfte	The president sent more armed forces to the war zone.	= military forces, soldiers
attitude	Haltung, Einstellung	Party members often have different attitudes.	= view, opinion
bill	Gesetzentwurf	The Senate discussed a new education bill.	= law
campaign	Wahlkampf	The parties started their campaign for the next election.	
(to) cast (a vote)	abstimmen	When you are 18 you can cast your vote for the first time.	= (to) vote
ceremony	Feier, Zeremonie	In a ceremony in Tucson more than 1,000 people became US citizens.	
challenge (to) challenge	Herausforderung herausfordern	The fight against poverty is a great challenge for the government.	
challenger	Herausforderer/Herausforderin		= rival, competitor

vocabulary	dt. Bedeutung	English sentence	syn/opp
charity	*wohltätige Zwecke Wohltätigkeit (-sorganisation)*	The millionaire gave all his money to charity. The Red Cross is a charity organisation.	
citizen	*Staatsbürger/-in*	Andy Garcia was born on the Island of Cuba, but he is an American citizen.	
city council	*Stadtrat*	The city council decided to pull down old houses in the centre.	
commission	*Kommission, Ausschuss*	A commission will look into the problems of single parents.	
committee	*Ausschuss*	A committee will work out the programme for the open day at our school.	
Congress [AE]	*Kongress*	The US Congress meets in the Capitol in Washington.	
(to) conquer	*erobern*	In 1066 William of Normandy conquered England.	
conquest	*Eroberung*	We talked about the Norman conquest.	
constitution	*Verfassung*	Great Britain does not have a written constitution. Germany has one and it is called the "Grundgesetz".	= fundamental law
council flat	*Sozialwohnung*	The government gives teenage mothers a free council flat if they go back to school.	
court	*Gericht*	You must tell the truth in court.	
death penalty	*Todesstrafe*	Many people are against the death penalty.	= capital punishment

vocabulary	dt. Bedeutung	English sentence	syn/opp
declaration (to) declare	*Erklärung erklären, verkünden, bekanntmachen*	The US Congress made a declaration of war in 1917.	
Declaration of Independence	*Unabhängigkeitserklärung*	The Declaration of Independence was written by the thirteen American colonies in 1776.	
(to) demonstrate demonstration	*demonstrieren* *Demonstration*	A lot of people demonstrated against the new law.	
department	*Ministerium, Abteilung*	My uncle works in a state department.	
district	*Gebiet, Bezirk*	Brixton is a district in South London where many black people live.	
duty	*Dienst, Pflicht*	The other police officer is on night duty this week.	
election (to) elect	*Wahl wählen*	In Germany, there is an election to the Bundestag every four years.	
emergency	*Notfall*	In case of an emergency, please pull this chain!	
European Union	*Europäische Union*	What do you know about the history of the European Union (EU)?	
execution (to) execute	*Hinrichtung hinrichten*	Texas is one of the US states with the highest number of executions.	
extract	*Auszug*	The students had to learn an extract from the Declaration of Independence.	= excerpt, passage
government (to) govern	*Regierung regieren*	The government must help people who cannot find work.	

vocabulary	dt. Bedeutung	English sentence	syn/opp
head of state	*Staatsoberhaupt*	The US president is head of state and also head of the government.	
independent	*unabhängig*	The American colonies wanted to be independent.	≠ dependent
independence	*Unabhängigkeit*		≠ dependence
(to be) involved	*beteiligt / eingebunden (sein)*	Mary and Harry are involved in the politics in their hometown.	
issue	*Streitfrage, Thema*	Crime and drugs are important issues today.	= problem
(to) join	*beitreten, mitmachen*	Would you like to join a political party?	≠ (to) quit
law	*Gesetz*	The government passed a new law which helps working mothers.	
lawyer	*Rechtsanwalt / Rechtsanwältin*	I'll have to ask my lawyer before I say anything more.	
(to) make a difference	*etwas ausmachen, einen Unterschied machen*	It does make a difference whether you go to an election or not.	
(to) make a speech	*eine Rede halten*	After her arrival at Philadelphia airport the Queen made a speech.	= (to) deliver / give a speech
mayor	*Bürgermeister/-in*	The mayor will visit our youth club next Saturday.	
Member of Parliament (MP)	*Parlamentsabgeordnete(r)*	In Britain there are more than 600 Members of Parliament / MPs.	
minister	*Minister/-in*	The environment minister said, "We have to reduce pollution."	
monarchy	*Monarchie*	Most British people want to keep the monarchy.	≠ republic

vocabulary	dt. Bedeutung	English sentence	syn/opp
nationality	*Nationalität*	Marc has double nationality: he has a German and a British passport.	
(to) nominate	*nominieren, ernennen*	The students nominated a girl and two boys for the position of class representative.	
nomination	*Nominierung, Ernennung*		
(to) overwhelm	*überwältigen*	The Conservatives won by an overwhelming majority.	
overwhelming	*überwältigend*		
(to) pass a law	*ein Gesetz verabschieden*	Congress passed a new law on immigration.	
platform	*Parteiprogramm, Wahlplattform*	The Democratic Party worked out a new platform for the coming election.	= programme
policy	*Politik, Taktik*	I do not agree with the government's housing policy.	
politician	*Politiker/-in*	Film star Arnold Schwarzenegger decided to become a politician.	
politics	*Politik*	Are you interested in politics?	
political	*politisch*		
power	*Macht*	It is not yet clear who will be in power after the next elections.	
president	*Präsident/-in*	The US president is head of the government and head of state.	
(to) preside	*den Vorsitz haben*		
presidential	*Präsidenten-, Präsidentschafts-*	In the USA presidential elections are held every four years.	
previous	*vorherig, vorhergehend*	The prime minister blamed the previous government for the bad economic situation of the country.	= former

vocabulary	dt. Bedeutung	English sentence	syn/opp
prime minister	*Premier-minister/-in*	Margaret Thatcher was Britain's first woman Prime Minister.	
process	*Prozess, Verfahren, Vorgang*	The peace process has come to a standstill.	
public	*Öffentlichkeit*	The general public is against higher taxes.	
regulation	*Vorschrift*	There are no government regulations about religious services at school.	
(to) represent representative	*vertreten Vertreter/-in*	The president represents the country abroad.	
resident (to) reside	*Bewohner/-in, Einwohner/-in wohnen*	My friend Shail's father comes from India. He has been a resident in Britain for 25 years.	
right to vote	*Stimmrecht*	Until 1965, many African Americans did not have the right to vote.	= suffrage, franchise
royal	*königlich, Königs-*	People all over the world are interested in the latest news about the British Royal Family.	
(to) run for president	*für das Präsidentenamt kandidieren*	Who do you think will run for president in the next election?	
Senate	*Senat*	There are 100 senators in the US Senate.	
session	*Sitzung, Sitzungsperiode*	The Members of Parliament discussed the new bill during their last session.	= meeting, conference

vocabulary	dt. Bedeutung	English sentence	syn/opp
society	*Gesellschaft*	There are too many poor people in today's society.	
	Verein	Ben and I joined our city's Historical Society.	
social	*gesellschaftlich*		
suburb	*Vorort, Stadt-randsiedlung*	Many people prefer living in a suburb to living in the noisy city centre.	≠ city centre, downtown
Supreme Court	*das Oberste Gericht*	The offices of the US Supreme Court are in Washington, D.C.	
tax	*Steuer*	There is a high tax on petrol and tobacco.	
term (of office)	*Amtszeit*	The president of the United States can only serve two terms of office.	
town hall	*Rathaus*	The athletes who had won an Olympic medal were invited to a celebration in the town hall.	
trial	*Prozess*	A lot of journalists were in the courtroom to watch the trial.	
(to) vote	*abstimmen, wählen*	When you are 18 you have the right to vote.	
vote	*Abstimmung, Wahl*		

Alphabetische Liste wichtiger Wörter

(to) abandon	aufgeben, preisgeben, verlassen	(to) admit	zulassen, zugeben, zugestehen
ability	Fähigkeit	(to) adopt	adoptieren, die Patenschaft übernehmen (für); übernehmen
(to be) able	fähig (sein)		
(to) abolish	abschaffen		
abroad	ins/im Ausland	adoption	Adoption; Übernahme
access	Zugang	adult	Erwachsene(r)
accommodation	Unterkunft	(to) advance	voranschreiten
account	Benutzerkonto	adventure	Abenteuer
(to) achieve	erreichen, leisten	(to) advertise	inserieren, werben
achievement	Leistung, Erfolg, Errungenschaft	advertisement (ad or advert)	Anzeige
(to) act	handeln	advertising	Werbung, Reklame
action	Handlung	advice	Rat
active	aktiv, lebhaft	(to) advise	raten
activity	Beschäftigung, Aktivität	(to) affect	sich auswirken auf, betreffen
actor, actress	Schauspieler, Schauspielerin	(to) afford	sich etwas leisten (können)
addicted	süchtig	(to be) afraid	befürchten
addiction	Sucht	African American	Afro-Amerikaner/-in
admiration	Bewunderung		
(to) admire	bewundern	against	gegen
admission	Zulassung, Eintritt	(to) agree	zustimmen, übereinstimmen

agreement	Vereinbarung, Übereinkunft
(to) allow	erlauben
alternative	Alternative, andere Möglichkeit
(to) amaze	erstaunen
amazement	Erstaunen
amazing	erstaunlich
amusement	Spaß, Unterhaltung
amusing	unterhaltsam
ancestor	Vorfahr(e)/Vorfahrin
anger	Zorn, Ärger, Wut
angry	zornig, wütend
annual	jährlich, Jahres-
answering machine	Anrufbeantworter
anxiety	Angst, Besorgnis
anxious	besorgt
apartment [AE]	Wohnung
(to) appear	erscheinen
appearance	Erscheinung, Aussehen
appliance	Gerät
app(lication)	Anwendung, App, Programm
application	Bewerbung
(to) apply	sich bewerben; beantragen
apprentice	Lehrling, Auszubildende(r)
apprenticeship	Lehrzeit, Lehre, Ausbildung
area	Gebiet, Bereich
(to) argue	argumentieren; sich streiten, zanken
argument	Argument; Wortwechsel, Streit
(to) arise	sich ergeben, entstehen
(to) arrest	festnehmen, verhaften
arrival	Ankunft
(to) arrive	ankommen
article	Artikel
artificial	künstlich
ashamed	beschämt
(to) ask for	bitten um
(to) assemble	sich versammeln
assembly	Versammlung
assignment	Aufgabe, Hausaufgabe
(to) assume	glauben, annehmen
(to) assure	versichern, zusichern, beteuern
athlete	Athlet/-in

atmosphere	Atmosphäre	bed and breakfast	Übernachtung mit Frühstück
(to) attack	angreifen	(to) behave	sich benehmen
attack	Angriff	(to) belong	gehören (zu), angehören
(to) attempt	versuchen		
attempt	Versuch	below	unten, unter
(to) attend	besuchen, anwesend sein	(to) bet	wetten
		bill	Gesetzentwurf
attitude	Haltung, Einstellung	birth	Geburt
(to) attract	anziehen	(to) give birth	zur Welt bringen
attraction	Anziehungskraft	birthday	Geburtstag
attractive	attraktiv, anziehend	birthplace	Geburtsort
audience	Publikum, Zuschauer	(to) blame	die Schuld geben, Vorwürfe machen
aunt	Tante		
available	verfügbar	blog	Blog, Internettagebuch
average	Durchschnitt; Durchschnitts-, durchschnittlich	(to) board	an Bord gehen, einsteigen
(to) avoid	vermeiden	boarding school	Internat
(to be) aware	(sich) bewusst (sein)	(to) boil	kochen, zum Kochen bringen
awful	schrecklich		
baggage [AE]	Gepäck	(to) book	buchen
balance	Gleichgewicht	booking	Reservierung, Buchung
(to) ban	verbieten		
ban	Verbot	border	Grenze
beach	Strand	(to be/feel) bored	gelangweilt (sein)
because of	wegen	boredom	Langeweile

boring	langweilig
(to) borrow	(aus-)leihen, entleihen
box office	Kino-, Theaterkasse
brain	Gehirn
(to) bring up	großziehen, erziehen
Briton	Brite/Britin
(to) broadcast	senden, übertragen
brochure	Broschüre
(to) bully	mobben, schikanieren
bully	gemeine(r) Mitschüler/-in
bullying	Mobbing, Schikanieren
business	Geschäft
busy	belebt, geschäftig
button	Knopf
(to) camp	zelten, lagern
campaign	Werbefeldzug; Wahlkampf
campsite	Campingplatz
camping van	Wohnmobil
cancer	Krebs
capital	Hauptstadt
carbon dioxide	Kohlendioxid
care	Sorge, Sorgfalt
(to) care for	sich kümmern um

(to) take care of	sich kümmern um, Sorge tragen für
career	berufliche Laufbahn, Karriere
careful	sorgfältig, vorsichtig
catastrophe	Katastrophe
(to) cause	verursachen
cause	Grund, Anlass
(to) celebrate	feiern
celebration	Feier, Fest
cell phone [AE]	Handy, Mobiltelefon
century	Jahrhundert
ceremony	Feier, Zeremonie
certificate	Urkunde
chain	Kette
(to) challenge	herausfordern
challenge	Herausforderung
champion	Sieger/-in, Champion
championship	Meisterschaft
channel	(Fernseh-)Kanal, Programm
charge	Verantwortung
(to be) in charge of	verantwortlich (sein) für
charity	wohltätige Zwecke; Wohltätigkeit(-sor-ganisation)

(to) chat	chatten; plaudern
chat	(Online-)Chat; Unterhaltung
(to) cheat	schummeln, betrügen
(to) check	überprüfen, kontrollieren
(to) check in	sich anmelden
(to) cheer	anfeuern
chemistry	Chemie
childhood	Kindheit
choice	Auswahl, Wahl
(to) choose	wählen, auswählen
circle	Kreis
citizen	Staatsbürger/-in
civil right	Bürgerrecht
civil rights movement	Bürgerrechtsbewegung (in den USA)
clash	Zusammenstoß
classmate	Klassenkamerad/-in
(to) click (on) a button	auf eine Schaltfläche klicken
climate	Klima
climate change	Klimawandel
cloning	Klonen, Schaffung von erbgleichen Wesen
coast	Küste
comfort	Komfort
comfortable	bequem
(to) command	befehlen, gebieten
(to) comment	sich äußern, einen Kommentar abgeben
commerce	Handel, Verkehr
commercial	Handels-, kaufmännisch, wirtschaftlich; Werbesendung, -spot
(to) communicate	etwas mitteilen
communication	Kommunikation
community	Gemeinde, Gemeinschaft
company	Firma
(to) compete	konkurrieren
competition	Wettbewerb
competitive	konkurrenzfähig
(to) complain	sich beklagen, sich beschweren
complaint	Beschwerde
complicated	kompliziert
composition	Aufsatz
comprehensive school	Gesamtschule
compulsory	obligatorisch, verpflichtend

computer scientist	Informatiker/-in	couple	(Ehe-)Paar
concerned	besorgt, betroffen	court	Gericht
(to) connect	verbinden	cousin	Cousin/Cousine
connection	Verbindung	cover	Bucheinband
(to) conquer	erobern	(to) create	(er-)schaffen
conquest	Eroberung	creation	Erschaffung
constitution	Verfassung	creature	Geschöpf, Lebewesen
(to) consume	verbrauchen	credit card	Kreditkarte
consumer	Verbraucher/-in	crew	Besatzung, Mannschaft
consumption	Verbrauch	crime	Verbrechen
(to) contact	kontaktieren, Verbindung aufnehmen	critic	Kritiker/-in
contact	Verbindung, Kontakt	criticism	Kritik
(to) contain	enthalten	(to) criticise	kritisieren
contents	Inhalt	crowd	Menge
convenient	praktisch, bequem	crowded	(mit Menschen) überfüllt
(to) cook	kochen, eine Mahlzeit zubereiten	(to) cure	heilen
cooking	Essen, Mahlzeiten, Küche	cure	Heilung
		current	aktuell
(to) copy	abschreiben, kopieren	curriculum vitae (CV)	Lebenslauf
copy	(Zeitungs-/Buch-) Exemplar	customer	Kunde/Kundin
(to) correct	korrigieren	cyberbullying	Cybermobbing, Internetschikane
correction	Korrektur	(to) cycle	Rad fahren
countryside	Landschaft	cycling	Radfahren, Radsport

(to) damage	schädigen	dependence, dependency	Abhängigkeit
data	Daten, Angaben	dependent	abhängig
date	Datum; Verabredung	descendant	Nachkomme, Nachfahre/ Nachfahrin
date of birth	Geburtsdatum		
day out	(Tages-)Ausflug		
death penalty	Todesstrafe	desert	Wüste
(to) decide	(sich) entscheiden	(to) deserve	verdienen
decision	Entscheidung	(to) design	entwerfen, gestalten
declaration	Erklärung	design	Entwurf, Gestaltung
(to) declare	erklären, verkünden, bekanntmachen	desperate	verzweifelt
		destination	Reiseziel
defeat	Niederlage	(to) destroy	zerstören, vernichten
defence	Verteidigung	destruction	Zerstörung
(to) defend	verteidigen	destructive	zerstörerisch
(to) delay	(sich) verspäten, verzögern	(to) develop	(sich) entwickeln
		device	Gerät
(to) delete	löschen	(to) die out	aussterben
(to) demon- strate	demonstrieren	diet	Kost, Ernährung, Nahrung
demonstration	Demonstration	(to) be/go on a diet	eine Diät machen
denial	Verweigerung, Leugnen		
(to) deny	verweigern, leugnen	(to) differ	sich unterscheiden
(to) depart	abfahren, abreisen	difference	Unterschied
departure	Abreise, Abfahrt	different	unterschiedlich, verschieden, anders
(to) depend on	abhängen von, abhängig sein von	dinner	Abendessen, Abendbrot

disadvantage	Nachteil	divorced	geschieden
(to) be at a disadvantage	benachteiligt sein	(to) do one's homework	Hausaufgaben machen
(to) disagree	nicht zustimmen	(to) do sport	Sport treiben
disagreement	Uneinigkeit	(to) do well	gut abschneiden
(to) disappear	verschwinden	(to) draw	anziehen, ziehen
disappearance	Verschwinden	drive (in a computer)	Laufwerk
disaster	Unglück, Katastrophe		
(to) discover	entdecken	(to) drive a car	Auto fahren
discovery	Entdeckung	driving licence	Führerschein
(to) discriminate	benachteiligen	(to) drop out of school	die Schule abbrechen/ vorzeitig verlassen
discrimination	unterschiedliche Behandlung, Benachteiligung	drought	Dürre
		drug	Droge, Rauschgift; Medikament
disease	Krankheit		
dish	Gericht; Schale, Schüssel, Platte; Satellitenschüssel	(to) dump	abladen, ablagern
		dump(ing ground)	Müllhalde, -kippe
(to) dismiss	entlassen, (jmdm.) kündigen	duty	Dienst, Pflicht
		(to) earn (one's living)	(seinen Lebensunter- halt) verdienen
distance	Entfernung		
distant	fern	earthquake	Erdbeben
(to) distract	ablenken	(to) educate	erziehen, ausbilden
(to) distribute	verteilen	educated	gebildet
distribution	Verteilung, Vertrieb	education	Ausbildung, Bildung
district	Gebiet, Bezirk	(to) effect	bewirken
divorce	Scheidung	effect	Wirkung, Auswirkung

effective	wirkungsvoll	enjoyment	Freude, Vergnügen
effort	Anstrengung	(to) enter	betreten, eintreten; teilnehmen an; eingeben
(to) elect	wählen		
election	Wahl	(to) entertain	unterhalten
electricity	Elektrizität	entertainment	Unterhaltung
emergency	Notfall	entrance	Eintritt, Zugang, Eingang
emigrant	Auswanderer/ Auswanderin		
		entry	Zugang, Zutritt
(to) emigrate	auswandern	environment	Umwelt
emigration	Auswanderung	environmentalist	Umweltschützer/-in
emission	Ausstoß	environmentally aware	umweltbewusst
(to) employ	beschäftigen, anstellen		
		environmentally friendly	umweltfreundlich
employee	Arbeitnehmer/-in, Angestellte(r)		
		equal	gleich
employer	Arbeitgeber/-in	equality	Gleichheit
employment	Beschäftigung, Arbeit	equal opportu- nities [Pl.]	Chancengleichheit
(to) encourage	ermutigen, Mut zusprechen		
		equal pay	gleiche Bezahlung
energy	Energie	(to) equip	ausstatten
engine	Motor	equipment	Ausrüstung
engineer	Ingenieur/-in, Konstrukteur/-in	essay	Aufsatz
		ethnic	ethnisch, Volks-
engineering	Ingenieurwesen, Maschinenbau	ethnic minority	ethnische Minderheit
		European Union	Europäische Union
(to) enjoy	genießen	event	Ereignis
enjoyable	angenehm		

evolution	Entwicklung, Evolution	factory	Fabrik
(to) evolve	sich entwickeln	(to) fail	nicht bestehen, durchfallen
exam	Prüfung	failure	Versagen, Misserfolg
exchange programme	Austauschprogramm	fair	Messe, Markt, Jahrmarkt
exchange visit	Schüleraustausch	fame	Ruhm
excited	aufgeregt	familiar	vertraut
excitement	Aufregung	family member	Familienmitglied, Angehörige(r)
exciting	aufregend	famous	berühmt
excursion	Ausflug	fashion	Mode
(to) go on an excursion	einen Ausflug machen	fashionable	modisch, schick
(to) exercise	trainieren, üben	fat	Fett
exercise	(körperliche) Bewegung, Training	(to) be in favour of	befürworten, dafür sein
exercise book	Heft	favourable	positiv, günstig, sympathisch
exhaust fumes	(Auto-)Abgase	favourite	Lieblings-
(to) experience	erleben	feedback	Rückmeldung
experience	Erlebnis, Erfahrung	female	weiblich
expert	Fachmann/Fachfrau	ferry	Fähre
exploration	Erforschung	festival	Festspiel, Festival
(to) explore	erkunden, erforschen	(to) fight	kämpfen
explorer	Forscher/-in	fight	Kampf
(to) extend	ausweiten	file	Datei
extra classes	Nachhilfe		
extract	Auszug		

(to) finish (school)	*(die Schule) beenden*
(to) flee	*fliehen*
flight	*Flug; Flucht*
(to) fly	*fliegen*
folder	*Verzeichnis, Ordner*
(to) forbid	*verbieten*
foreign	*ausländisch*
foreigner	*Ausländer/-in*
foreign language	*Fremdsprache*
form teacher	*Klassenlehrer/-in*
fortunate	*glücklich, vom Schicksal begünstigt*
fortune	*Vermögen; Schicksal*
fossil fuel	*fossiler Brennstoff*
freedom of expression	*Meinungsfreiheit*
freedom of the press	*Pressefreiheit*
frontier	*Grenze, Grenzgebiet*
full-time	*Vollzeit, ganztägig, Ganztags-*
(to) function	*funktionieren*
(to) gain	*gewinnen, erlangen*
gap year	*freies Jahr (meist zwischen dem Schulabschluss und dem Beginn des Studiums)*
GCSE (= General Certificate of Secondary Education)	*Schulabschluss (entspricht in etwa dem deutschen Realschulabschluss)*
gene	*Gen*
genetic engineering	*Gentechnik*
(to) get away	*entfliehen, entkommen*
(to) get rid of	*loswerden*
gift shop	*Geschenkartikelladen*
global	*global, weltweit*
global warming	*Erderwärmung*
goal	*Ziel, Tor*
goalkeeper	*Torwart/-in, Torhüter/-in*
(to) govern	*regieren*
government	*Regierung*
(to) graduate	*die Abschlussprüfung bestehen, abgehen von*
graduate	*Absolvent/-in, Abgänger/-in*
grammar school	*Gymnasium*
grandchild	*Enkel/-in*
granddaughter	*Enkelin*
grandparents	*Großeltern*
grandson	*Enkel*
(to) guard	*bewachen*

guard	Wächter/-in	Hispanics	Hispano-Amerikaner
guidance	Leitung, Führung	holiday job	Ferienarbeit
(to) guide	führen, leiten	holiday maker	Urlauber/-in
guide	(Fremden-)Führer/-in, Reiseleiter/-in	holiday resort	Ferienort
guidebook	Reiseführer (Buch)	homeland	Heimatland, Vaterland
habit	Gewohnheit	homeless	obdachlos
(to) harm	schädigen	hospital	Krankenhaus
harmful	schädlich	host	Gastgeber/-in
(to) hate	hassen	host family	Gastfamilie
hate, hatred	Hass	hostile	feindlich
headache	Kopfschmerzen	hostility	Feindschaft, Feindseligkeit
heading	Überschrift	household	Haushalt
headline	Schlagzeile	housework	Hausarbeit
headmaster	Schulleiter, Direktor	(to) do housework	Hausarbeit machen
headmistress	Schulleiterin, Direktorin	human	menschlich
head of state	Staatsoberhaupt	human being	Mensch
health	Gesundheit	human rights	Menschenrechte
health care	Gesundheitsfürsorge	husband	Ehemann
healthy	gesund	illegal	illegal, ungesetzlich, rechtswidrig
hereditary	Erb-	immigrant	Einwanderer/Einwanderin
heritage	Erbe		
high school [AE]	weiterführende Schule, Highschool	(to) immigrate	einwandern
(to) hire	mieten	immigration	Einwanderung

importance	Bedeutung, Wichtigkeit
important	wichtig
(to) improve	(sich) verbessern, besser machen/ werden
improvement	Verbesserung
income	Einkommen, Einkünfte
(to) increase	steigern, erhöhen, zunehmen
increase	Erhöhung, Zunahme
increasing	zunehmend, steigend
independence	Unabhängigkeit
independent	unabhängig
individual	individuell, persönlich
indoors	drinnen
industrial	industriell
industry	Industrie(-zweig), Gewerbe
infant school [BE]	Vorschule, Spielschule
(to) infect	infizieren, anstecken
infection	Ansteckung
(to) inhabit	bewohnen
(to) inherit	erben
inheritance	Erbe
(to) injure	verletzen
injury	Verletzung
(to) install	aufstellen, installieren
interest	Interesse
(to) be interested in	sich interessieren für
(on the) internet	(im) Internet
(to) interrupt	unterbrechen
(to) intimidate	einschüchtern, Angst einjagen
(to) introduce	einführen
introduction	Einführung, Einleitung
(to) invent	erfinden
invention	Erfindung
inventor	Erfinder/-in
(to be) involved	beteiligt / einge- bunden (sein)
(to) isolate	isolieren
isolated	einsam
isolation	Isolation
issue	(Zeitungs-)Ausgabe, Nummer; Streitfrage, Thema
jealous	eifersüchtig
jealousy	Eifersucht
job	Beruf, Beschäftigung, Stelle
job experience	Berufserfahrung

job interview	Vorstellungsgespräch	leisure (time)	Freizeit
(to) join	beitreten, mitmachen	lesson	Unterrichtsstunde, Lektion
journey	Reise		
junk food	minderwertiges, ungesundes Essen	level	Niveau, Ebene
		liberty	Freiheit
(to) keep fit	fit, gesund bleiben	library	Bücherei, Bibliothek
(to) keep in touch	in Verbindung bleiben	lifestyle	Lebensstil, Lebensweise
key	Taste	(to) limit	begrenzen
keyboard	Tastatur	limit	Grenze
labour	Arbeit, Arbeitskräfte	limitation	Begrenzung
lake	See	(to) listen (to music / to the radio)	(Musik/Radio) hören
landline	Festnetz		
landmark	Wahrzeichen	live [ai]	direkt, live
lane	Spur	(to) live on	leben von
language	Sprache	lost property office	Fundbüro
language course	Sprachkurs		
(to) last	dauern	lunch	Mittagessen
latest	neueste(r/s)	(to) maintain	aufrechterhalten, bewahren
(to) launch	(eine Rakete usw.) starten; mit etwas beginnen	maintenance	Bewahrung; Wartung
		majority	Mehrheit
launch	Start	(to) make a difference	etwas ausmachen, einen Unterschied machen
law	Gesetz		
lawyer	Rechtsanwalt/ Rechtsanwältin	(to) make a speech	eine Rede halten
(to) leave	verlassen	(to) manage	(etwas) fertigbringen

manager	Manager/-in; Trainer/-in	message	Nachricht, Botschaft, Mitteilung
(to) manufacture	herstellen, erzeugen	migration	Migration, Wanderung
manufacturer	Hersteller	(to) mind	ausmachen
(to) mark	benoten, bewerten, korrigieren	minimum wage	Mindestlohn
mark	Schulnote	minister	Minister/-in
marriage	Heirat, Ehe	minority	Minderheit
(to) marry	heiraten	minute	Minute; winzig
mass media	Massenmedien	misery	Elend, Not
match	Spiel	(to) miss	verpassen
maths	Mathe	(to) mix	mischen
mayor	Bürgermeister/-in	mixture	Mischung, Gemisch
meal	Mahlzeit	mobile (phone)	Handy, Mobiltelefon
means	Mittel	(to) modify	ändern
means of communication	Kommunikationsmittel	monarchy	Monarchie
means of transport	Verkehrsmittel, Beförderungsmittel	multi-ethnic	multiethnisch, Menschen verschiedener Herkunft umfassend
meeting	Versammlung, Besprechung, Treffen	muscle	Muskel
member	Mitglied	musician	Musiker/-in
Member of Parliament (MP)	Parlamentsabgeordnete(r)	mysterious	rätselhaft, geheimnisvoll
membership	Mitgliedschaft	mystery	Geheimnis
menu	Speisekarte	nationality	Nationalität
		national park	Nationalpark

native	einheimisch; (Ur-)Einwohner/-in
native Americans	Indianer, amerikanische Ureinwohner
native language	Muttersprache
native speaker	Muttersprachler/-in
neighbour	Nachbar/-in
neighbourhood	Nachbarschaft, Viertel
nephew	Neffe
network	Netz, Netzwerk
newcomer	Neuankömmling
news	Nachricht(en)
niece	Nichte
nightmare	Alptraum
(to) nominate	nominieren, ernennen
nomination	Nominierung, Ernennung
non-violent	gewaltlos
nuclear power plant	Atomkraftwerk
obesity	Fettleibigkeit
obese	übergewichtig
(to) object to	Einspruch erheben gegen
(to) offer	anbieten
offer	Angebot
Olympic Games	Olympische Spiele
(to) oppose	sich wenden gegen, gegen etwas sein
opposite	Gegenteil; gegenüber, entgegengesetzt
opposition	Widerstand
oppressed	unterdrückt
oppression	Unterdrückung
oral	mündlich
(to) order	bestellen
order	Bestellung, Auftrag
origin	Ursprung, Herkunft
original	ursprünglich
orphan	Waise(-nkind)
outdoors	im Freien
(to) overcome	überwinden, bewältigen
overseas	Auslands-, ausländisch
(to) overtake	überholen
overtime	Überstunden
overweight	übergewichtig
(to) overwhelm	überwältigen
overwhelming	überwältigend
package holiday	Pauschalurlaub
(to) paint	malen
paragraph	(Text-)Absatz

particularly	besonders, vor allem	petrol [BE]	Benzin
part-time	Teilzeit-, Halbtags-	physical	körperlich
(to) pass	(eine Prüfung) bestehen; (ein Gesetz) verabschieden	physics	Physik
		(to) play a musical instrument	ein Musikinstrument spielen
passenger	Passagier, Fluggast		
passport	Reisepass	(to) play chess	Schach spielen
pastime	Zeitvertreib	(to) play on the computer	am Computer spielen
patchwork family	Familie, in der Kinder von verschiedenen Eltern aufwachsen	pleasant	angenehm
		(to) please	gefallen
pay(ment)	Bezahlung, Lohn	pleasure	Vergnügen
PE (= Physical Education)	Sportunterricht	poison	Gift, Schadstoff
peace	Friede	poisonous	giftig
peaceful	friedlich	policy	Politik, Taktik
pen friend	Brieffreund/-in	political	politisch
perfect	vollkommen	politician	Politiker/-in
(to) perform	aufführen	politics	Politik
performance	Vorstellung, Auf- führung; Leistung	(to) pollute	verschmutzen
		polluting	umweltschädlich
(to) persecute	verfolgen	pollution	Verschmutzung
persecution	Verfolgung	poor	arm
perspective	Perspektive, Blickwinkel	popular	beliebt
		popularity	Beliebtheit
(to) persuade	überzeugen, überreden	(to) populate	bevölkern
persuasion	Überredung	population	Bevölkerung

position	Stellung	(to) produce	herstellen, erzeugen
poverty	Armut	production	Herstellung
power	Macht; Kraft, Stärke	professional	beruflich; Berufs-; Profisportler/-in
powerful	mächtig; stark	programme	Sendung
power station	Kraftwerk	(to) promote	fördern, für etwas werben; (jmdn.) befördern
(to) praise	loben		
pregnancy	Schwangerschaft		
pregnant	schwanger	promotion	Beförderung; Werbung, Werbekampagne
prejudice	Vorurteil		
(to) be preju-diced against	Vorurteile haben gegenüber	prospect	Aussicht, Chance
		(to) protect	schützen
(to) prepare	sich vorbereiten	protection	Schutz
president	Präsident/-in	(to) provide	zur Verfügung stellen, liefern
presidential	Präsidenten-, Präsidentschafts-		
		public	Öffentlichkeit; öffentlich
pressure	Druck		
(to) put pressure on	Druck ausüben auf	publication	Veröffentlichung
		public school [BE]	Privatschule
prestige	Ansehen		
previous	vorherig, vorhergehend	public transport	öffentliche Verkehrs-mittel
primary school	Grundschule	(to) publish	veröffentlichen, herausgeben
prime minister	Premierminister/-in		
(to) print	drucken	(to) punish	(be-)strafen
printer	Drucker	punishment	Strafe
process	Prozess, Verfahren, Vorgang	pupil	Schüler/-in

qualification	Qualifikation, Abschlusszeugnis; Eignung; Vorbildung
qualified	ausgebildet, qualifiziert
(to) qualify	sich qualifizieren
quality (news)paper	seriöse Tageszeitung
questionnaire	Fragebogen
(to) quit	(selbst) kündigen
race	„Rasse"; Wettlauf, Rennen
racial	„rassisch", „Rassen-"
racism	Rassismus
racist	Rassist/-in
rainforest	Regenwald
(to) raise	großziehen, aufziehen
raw material	Rohstoff
(to) receive	empfangen, erhalten
receiver	Empfänger
reception	Empfang
receptionist	Empfangschef, Empfangsdame (im Hotel)
recognition	(An-)Erkennung
(to) recognise	erkennen
(to) recommend	empfehlen
recommendation	Empfehlung
(to) record	aufzeichnen, aufnehmen
(to) recycle	recyceln, wieder aufbereiten
recycling	Wiederverwertung
(to) reduce	verringern
reduction	Verringerung
refugee	Flüchtling
regional	regional
regulation	Vorschrift
rehearsal	Probe
(to) rehearse	proben
relationship	Beziehung
relative	Verwandte(r)
(to) relax	sich entspannen
(to) release	freisetzen, freilassen
(to) rely on	sich verlassen auf
renewable	erneuerbar
(to) rent	mieten, leihen
(to) repair	reparieren
(to) repeat	wiederholen
(to) report	berichten
report	Bericht
(to) represent	vertreten

representative	Vertreter/-in	(to) retire	in Pension/Rente gehen, sich pensionieren lassen
reputation	Ruf		
(to) request	bitten	retirement	Rente, Pension
request	Bitte, Wunsch	reusable	wiederverwertbar
(to) research	forschen	(to) reuse	wiederverwenden
research	Forschung	review	Rezension, Kritik
researcher	Forscher/-in	(to) ride a bike	Rad fahren
reservation	Reservierung	right to vote	Stimmrecht
(to) reserve	reservieren	riot	(Straßen-)Schlacht, Krawall
(to) reside	wohnen		
resident	Bewohner/-in, Einwohner/-in	rival	Konkurrent/-in
		rocket	Rakete
(to) resign	zurücktreten	role	Rolle
resignation	Kündigung	roof	Dach
(to) resist	sich widersetzen	route	Route, Strecke
resistance	Widerstand	royal	königlich, Königs-
resort	Urlaubsort, Ferienort	rubbish [BE]	Müll, Abfall
resources	Bodenschätze, Ressourcen	rule	Bestimmung, Verbot, Vorschrift
respect	Achtung, Respekt; Hinsicht, Beziehung	(to) run a firm	eine Firma leiten
respectable	anständig	(to) run for president	für das Präsidentenamt kandidieren
respected	geachtet	rush hour	Hauptverkehrszeit
respectively	beziehungsweise	safe	sicher
(to) restrict	beschränken, einschränken	safety	Sicherheit
restriction	Ein-, Beschränkung	salary	Gehalt (Geld)

sale	*Verkauf*	seat belt	*Sicherheitsgurt*
same-sex marriage	*gleichgeschlechtliche Ehe*	secondary school [BE]	*weiterführende Schule*
(to) save	*sparen; retten; (eine Datei) sichern, speichern*	secret	*Geheimnis*
		secure	*sicher*
(to) scare	*erschrecken*	security	*Sicherheit, Sicherheitsvor- kehrungen*
scenery	*Landschaft*		
school fees	*Schulgeld, Schul- gebühren*	(to) see	*sehen*
		segregation	*Rassentrennung*
school holiday(s) [BE]	*Schulferien*	(to) sell	*verkaufen*
school-leaving certificate	*Abgangszeugnis*	(to) separate [eit]	*(sich) trennen, (ab)teilen*
school trip	*Schulfahrt, Klassen- reise*	separate [it]	*getrennt, abgesondert*
school uniform	*Schuluniform*	series	*Serie*
school yard	*Schulhof*	serious	*ernst, ernsthaft*
science	*Naturwissenschaft*	(to) set out	*aufbrechen*
scientific	*wissenschaftlich*	(to) settle	*sich niederlassen, besiedeln*
scientist	*Naturwissen- schaftler/-in, Wissen- schaftler/-in*	settlement	*Siedlung, Nieder- lassung*
screen	*Bildschirm*	settler	*Siedler/-in*
sea level	*Meeresspiegel*	shelter	*Schutz, Schutzraum*
(to) search	*suchen*	shift	*(Arbeits-)Schicht*
search	*Suche*	shopping trip	*Einkaufstour*
search engine	*Suchmaschine*	(to) shorten	*verkürzen*
seaside resort	*Seebad*	(to) shout	*schreien*

sight	Sehenswürdigkeit	soft drink	alkoholfreies Getränk
sightseeing	Besichtigung(en)	solar	Solar-, Sonnen-
(to) go sightseeing	auf Besichtigungstour gehen	solar energy	Sonnenenergie
(to) sign a contract	einen Vertrag unterschreiben	solution	Lösung
		(to) solve	lösen, auflösen
single	ledig	source	Quelle
single mother/father	alleinerziehende(r) Mutter/Vater	space	Weltraum, Raum
		spaceship	Raumschiff
single parent	Alleinerziehende(r)	space travel	Raumfahrt
single room	Einzelzimmer	spare time	Freizeit
(to) sit a paper	eine Klausur schreiben	spare-time activity	Freizeitbeschäftigung
site	Ort, Platz	spectacular	atemberaubend, fantastisch
skilful	erfahren, geschickt		
skill	Fähigkeit, Fertigkeit, Qualifikation	spectator	Zuschauer/-in
		speed limit	Geschwindigkeits-begrenzung
skilled	ausgebildet, qualifiziert; gelernt	(to) spell	(richtig) schreiben, buchstabieren
slavery	Sklaverei		
slogan	Werbespruch	spelling	Rechtschreibung; Rechtschreib-
(to) slow down	verringern, verlangsamen	(to) spend	verbringen
soccer [AE]	(europäischer) Fuß-ball	(to) sponsor	sponsern, finanziell unterstützen
social	gesellschaftlich	sponsor	Sponsor/-in, Förderer/Förderin
social media	soziale Medien		
society	Gesellschaft; Verein	sports event	Sportveranstaltung

sportsman, sportswoman	Sportler, Sportlerin
(to) spread	ausbreiten, sich verbreiten
staff	Belegschaft
standard of living	Lebensstandard
(to) start a family	eine Familie gründen
state school	staatliche Schule
stay	Aufenthalt
(to) stay at a hotel	in einem Hotel wohnen
(to) stay on	länger (in der Schule) bleiben
still	noch
stressful	anstrengend, aufreibend, stressig
strict	streng
strike	Streik
(to) study	studieren
subject	Schulfach
suburb	Vorort, Stadtrandsiedlung
(to) succeed	Erfolg haben
success	Erfolg
successful	erfolgreich
supper	Abendessen
(to) support a family	eine Familie ernähren

supporter	Anhänger/-in, Fan
surface	Oberfläche
(to) surf the internet	im Internet surfen
survival	Überleben
(to) survive	überleben
(to) switch off	ausschalten
tabloid	Boulevardzeitung, Klatschzeitung
(to) take a break	eine Pause machen
(to) take an exam	eine Prüfung machen
(to) take part in	teilnehmen an
(to) take place	stattfinden
(to) take off	starten
take-off	Start (eines Flugzeugs)
talent	Begabung
talented	begabt
(to) taste	schmecken
taste	Geschmack
tasty	lecker
tax	Steuer
technical	technisch, fachlich, Fach-
technology	Technologie

television set (TV set)	*Fernsehapparat*	(to) trace	*aufspüren, ausfindig machen, finden*
tense	*gespannt, spannend*	trade	*Handel, Handelsverkehr; Beruf (im Handwerk)*
tension	*Spannung*		
terrible	*schrecklich*	traffic	*Verkehr*
(to) text	*eine SMS/Kurznachricht schreiben*	traffic jam	*Verkehrsstau*
		(to) train	*trainieren*
text (message)	*SMS, Kurznachricht*	trainee	*Praktikant/-in, Azubi, Lehrling*
textbook	*Lehrbuch*		
threat	*Bedrohung*	trainer	*Trainer*
(to) threaten	*bedrohen*	training	*Ausbildung; Training*
ticket	*Karte*	(to) travel	*reisen*
tolerance	*Duldsamkeit, Toleranz*	travel agent	*Reiseberater/-in*
tolerant	*duldsam, tolerant*	travel agent's, travel agency	*Reisebüro*
(to) tolerate	*dulden, tolerieren*		
tongue	*Zunge*	traveller	*Reisende(r)*
tool	*Werkzeug, Gerät*	(to) treat	*behandeln*
tour	*Rundreise, Tour*	treatment	*Behandlung*
tourism	*Tourismus*	trend	*Trend, Richtung*
tourist attraction	*Sehenswürdigkeit, Touristenattraktion*	trendy	*modisch*
		trial	*Prozess*
tourist information	*Fremdenverkehrsamt*	tribe	*(Volks-)Stamm*
		trouble	*Problem, Schwierigkeit*
tournament	*Turnier*		
town hall	*Rathaus*	(to) turn down	*(Lautstärke) leiser stellen*

(to) turn off	*(Radio, Fernseher, Computer) ausschalten*	**vegan**	*Veganer/-in*
		vegetables	*Gemüse*
(to) turn on	*(Radio, Fernseher, Computer) an-, einschalten*	**vegetarian**	*vegetarisch; Vegetarier/-in*
(to) tweet	*twittern, einen Tweet schreiben*	**vehicle**	*Fahrzeug*
		victim	*Opfer*
twin	*Zwilling*	**victory**	*Sieg*
unemployed	*arbeitslos*	**viewer**	*(Fernseh-) Zuschauer/-in*
unemployment	*Arbeitslosigkeit*	**village**	*Dorf*
unit	*Lektion*	**violence**	*Gewalt, Gewalt- tätigkeit*
university	*Universität*		
unskilled	*ungelernt, nicht ausgebildet*	**violent**	*gewalttätig; heftig*
		virtual	*virtuell*
user	*Nutzer/-in, Anwender/-in*	**virus**	*Virus*
vacancy	*freie/offene Stelle*	**vocabulary**	*Wortschatz, Vokabular*
vacant	*frei*	**volume**	*Lautstärke; Band*
vacation [AE]	*Ferien*		
valley	*Tal*	**voluntary**	*freiwillig*
(to) vandalise	*zerstören*	**volunteer**	*Freiwillige(r)*
vandalism	*Zerstörungswut*	**(to) vote**	*abstimmen, wählen*
varied	*vielfältig*	**vote**	*Abstimmung, Wahl*
variety	*Vielfalt*	**wage**	*(Arbeits-)Lohn*
various	*vielfältig, verschieden*	**waiter, waitress**	*Kellner, Kellnerin*
(to) vary	*variieren, wechseln, schwanken*	**(to) warn**	*warnen*
		warning	*Warnung*

(to) waste	vergeuden	**work permit**	Arbeitserlaubnis
waste	Abfall	**(to) work shifts**	Schicht arbeiten
(to) watch TV/ television	fernsehen	**workshop**	Workshop, Seminar; Werkstatt
weak	schwach	**world championship**	Weltmeisterschaft
weakness	Schwäche		
(to) wear	(Kleidung) tragen	**(to) worry about**	sich sorgen, sich Sorgen machen (über)
wedding	Hochzeit		
(to) weigh	wiegen	**worry**	Sorge, Kummer
weight	Gewicht	**written test**	Klassenarbeit, schriftliche Arbeit
(to) lose weight	abnehmen		
welfare [AE]	Sozialhilfe	**xenophobia**	Ausländerfeindlich-keit
wife	Ehefrau		
wireless internet	WLAN, drahtloses Internet	**youth**	Jugendliche(r)
		youth centre/club	Jugendzentrum, -klub
work	Arbeit		
(to) be out of work	arbeitslos sein	**youth hostel**	Jugendherberge
working conditions	Arbeitsbedingungen		

Countries – People – Languages

Country	Inhabitant	Language
Australia	Australian	English
Austria	Austrian	German
Belgium	Belgian	Flemish / French
Brazil	Brazilian	Portuguese
Britain	Briton	English
Canada	Canadian	English / French
Denmark	Dane	Danish
England	Englishman/Englishwoman	English
Finland	Finn	Finnish / Swedish
France	Frenchman/Frenchwoman	French
Germany	German	German
Greece	Greek	Greek
Holland/the Netherlands	Dutchman/Dutchwoman	Dutch
Hungary	Hungarian	Hungarian
India	Indian	Hindi / English
Ireland	Irishman/Irishwoman	English / Gaelic
Italy	Italian	Italian
Japan	Japanese	Japanese
Mexico	Mexican	Spanish
New Zealand	New Zealander	English
Norway	Norwegian	Norwegian
Poland	Pole	Polish

Country	Inhabitant	Language
Portugal	a Portuguese man/woman	Portuguese
Russia	Russian	Russian
Scotland	Scotsman/Scotswoman	English / Gaelic
South Africa	South African	English / Afrikaans
Spain	Spaniard	Spanish
Sweden	Swede	Swedish
Switzerland	a Swiss man/woman	German / French / Italian
Turkey	Turk	Turkish
United Kingdom	Briton	English
USA	American	English
Wales	Welshman/Welshwoman	English / Gaelic

Britisches und amerikanisches Englisch

British English [BE]	American English [AE]	deutsche Bedeutung
autumn	fall	*Herbst*
bill	check	*Rechnung*
biscuit	cookie	*Keks*
chat show	talk show	*Talkshow*
chemist's	pharmacy, drugstore	*Apotheke*
chips [Pl.]	(French) fries [Pl.]	*Pommes frites*
cinema	movie theater	*Kino*
city centre	downtown	*City, Innenstadt*
crisps [Pl.]	potato chips [Pl.]	*Chips*
driving licence	driver's license	*Führerschein*
film	movie	*(Kino-)Film*
first floor	second floor	*1. Stock*
flat	apartment	*Wohnung*
football	soccer	*Fußball*
full stop	period, bei Internetadressen: dot	*Punkt*
ground floor	first floor	*Erdgeschoss*
handbag	purse, pocketbook	*Handtasche*
(to) hire a car	(to) rent a car	*ein Auto mieten*
holiday	vacation	*Urlaub*
holidays [Pl.]	vacation	*Schulferien*
jam	jelly	*Marmelade*
lift	elevator	*Aufzug*

British English [BE]	American English [AE]	deutsche Bedeutung
motorway	highway, freeway	*Autobahn*
note	bill	*Geldschein*
of course	sure	*natürlich*
Pardon? Sorry?	Excuse me?	*Wie bitte?*
pavement	sidewalk	*Bürgersteig*
petrol	gas, gasoline	*Benzin*
petrol station	gas station	*Tankstelle*
post-box	mailbox	*Briefkasten*
postcode	zip code	*Postleitzahl*
purse	wallet, coin purse	*Portemonnaie*
queue	line	*Warteschlange*
rails [Pl.]	tracks [Pl.]	*Gleis(e)*
railway	railroad	*Bahn*
shop	store	*Geschäft*
sorry	excuse me	*Entschuldigung!*
subway	(pedestrian) underpass	*Fußgängerunterführung*
sweet	candy	*Bonbon*
taxi	cab	*Taxi*
timetable	schedule	*Fahrplan*
toilet	bathroom, restroom	*W.C.*
torch	flashlight	*Taschenlampe*
trousers [Pl.]	pants [Pl.]	*Hose*
underground	subway	*U-Bahn*

Unregelmäßige Verben

Infinitive	Past Tense	Past Participle	deutsche Übersetzung
be	was/were	been	*sein*
bear	bore	born(e)	*(er)tragen; gebären*
beat	beat	beaten	*schlagen*
begin	began	begun	*beginnen*
bind	bound	bound	*binden*
bite	bit	bit(ten)	*beißen*
blow	blew	blown	*blasen*
break	broke	broken	*brechen*
bring	brought	brought	*bringen*
build	built	built	*bauen*
burn	burnt/ed	burnt/ed	*brennen*
buy	bought	bought	*kaufen*
catch	caught	caught	*fangen*
choose	chose	chosen	*wählen*
come	came	come	*kommen*
deal	dealt	dealt	*handeln*
do	did	done	*tun*
draw	drew	drawn	*zeichnen, ziehen*
dream	dreamt/ed	dreamt/ed	*träumen*
drink	drank	drunk	*trinken*
drive	drove	driven	*fahren*
eat	ate	eaten	*essen*

Infinitive	Past Tense	Past Participle	deutsche Übersetzung
fall	fell	fallen	*fallen*
feed	fed	fed	*füttern*
feel	felt	felt	*fühlen*
fight	fought	fought	*kämpfen*
find	found	found	*finden*
fly	flew	flown	*fliegen*
forbid	forbade	forbidden	*verbieten*
forget	forgot	forgotten	*vergessen*
forgive	forgave	forgiven	*vergeben*
freeze	froze	frozen	*frieren*
give	gave	given	*geben*
go	went	gone	*gehen*
grow	grew	grown	*wachsen*
hear	heard	heard	*hören*
hide	hid	hidden	*verstecken*
hold	held	held	*halten*
keep	kept	kept	*halten*
know	knew	known	*wissen*
lay	laid	laid	*legen*
lead	led	led	*leiten*
learn	learnt/ed	learnt/ed	*lernen*
leave	left	left	*(ver-)lassen*
lend	lent	lent	*leihen*
lean	leant/ed	leant/ed	*lehnen*
lie	lay	lain	*liegen*

Infinitive	Past Tense	Past Participle	deutsche
lose	lost	lost	*verlieren*
make	made	made	*machen*
mean	meant	meant	*meinen, bedeuten*
meet	met	met	*treffen*
pay	paid	paid	*bezahlen*
read [iː]	read [e]	read [e]	*lesen*
ride	rode	ridden	*fahren, reiten*
ring	rang	rung	*läuten*
rise	rose	risen	*aufstehen, aufgehen, ansteigen*
run	ran	run	*laufen, rennen*
say	said	said	*sagen*
see	saw	seen	*sehen*
seek	sought	sought	*suchen*
sell	sold	sold	*verkaufen*
send	sent	sent	*senden*
shake	shook	shaken	*schütteln*
shine	shone	shone	*scheinen*
shoot	shot	shot	*schießen*
show	showed	shown	*zeigen*
shrink	shrank	shrunk	*schrumpfen, einlaufen*
sing	sang	sung	*singen*
sink	sank	sunk	*sinken*
sit	sat	sat	*sitzen*
sleep	slept	slept	*schlafen*

		Past Participle	deutsche Übersetzung
	...elled	smelt/smelled	*riechen*
		spoken	*sprechen*
sp...	spelt	spelt	*buchstabieren*
spend	spent	spent	*verbringen, ausgeben*
spring	sprang	sprung	*springen*
stand	stood	stood	*stehen*
steal	stole	stolen	*stehlen*
stick	stuck	stuck	*kleben*
swear	swore	sworn	*schwören, fluchen*
sweep	swept	swept	*fegen*
swim	swam	swum	*schwimmen*
swing	swung	swung	*schwingen*
take	took	taken	*nehmen*
teach	taught	taught	*lehren*
tear	tore	torn	*reißen*
tell	told	told	*erzählen*
think	thought	thought	*denken, glauben*
throw	threw	thrown	*werfen*
understand	understood	understood	*verstehen*
wake	woke	woken	*aufwachen, wecken*
wear	wore	worn	*tragen*
win	won	won	*gewinnen*
write	wrote	written	*schreiben*

Liebe Kundin, lieber Kunde,

der STARK Verlag hat das Ziel, Sie effektiv beim Lernen zu unterstützen.
In welchem Maße uns dies gelingt, wissen Sie am besten. Deshalb bitten wir Sie,
uns Ihre Meinung zu den STARK-Produkten in dieser Umfrage mitzuteilen:

www.stark-verlag.de/feedback

Als Dankeschön verlosen wir einmal jährlich, zum 31. Juli, unter allen
Teilnehmern ein aktuelles Samsung-Tablet. Für nähere Informationen
und die Teilnahmebedingungen folgen Sie dem Internetlink.

Herzlichen Dank!

Haben Sie weitere Fragen an uns?
Sie erreichen uns telefonisch **08167 9573-0**
per E-Mail **info@stark-verlag.de**
oder im Internet unter **www.stark-verlag.de**

Erfolgreich durch alle Klassen mit den **STARK** Reihen